Two Millennia of Church and Community in Orkney

Two Millennia of Church and Community in Orkney

Frank Bardgett

The Pentland Press Limited
Edinburgh • Cambridge • Durham • USA

© Frank Bardgett 2000

First published in 2000 by
The Pentland Press Ltd.
1 Hutton Close
South Church
Bishop Auckland
Durham

All rights reserved.
Unauthorised duplication
contravenes existing laws.

British Library Cataloguing in Publication Data.
A Catalogue record for this book is available
from the British Library.

ISBN 1 85821 759 8

Typeset by CBS, Martlesham Heath, Ipswich, Suffolk
Printed and bound by Antony Rowe Ltd., Chippenham

CONTENTS

List of Illustrations		vii
Foreword	Church History and Community Ministry	ix
Chapter 1	The Mystery of the Prehistoric	1
2	The Celtic Missionaries: breadth and depth to the mystery	9
3	The 'Conversion' of the Norse: AD 995	33
4	Catholic and Protestant; Episcopalian and Presbyterian: 1540–1715	49
	Tables of the reformed Ministry in Orkney 1560–90	93
5	Secession, Disruption and Reunion: 1790–1929	101
Index:	People	143
Index:	Places	147

ILLUSTRATIONS

Standing Stone, Stoneyhill, Harray	2
The Stone of Setter, Eday	3
Symbol for the Scottish Churches' 'Year of Faith', 1997	9
Illustration based on an early Christian altar cross, Flotta	14
8th century Christian cross-slab found in the St Boniface Kirkyard, Papa Westray	14
Early Christian incised stone found on the Brough of Birsay	14
Early Christian incised cross, Broch of Burrian, North Ronaldsay	14
The Chapel on the Brough of Deerness	20
Pictish symbol stone	23
15th century statue of St Magnus from Kirkwall Cathedral	39
Seal of Adam Bothwell, Bishop of Orkney	55
The Covenanters' Memorial, Deerness	78
The 'Paterson Kirk', Kirkwall	104
Rev David Webster, minister of the United Presbyterian congregation, Kirkwall	113
Rev. Dr William Logie, minister, first charge, St Magnus Cathedral, Kirkwall	129

Foreword

Church History and Community Ministry

The people and places of history have fascinated me since I was a small boy. My first employment was teaching secondary history. While becoming a minister of the Church of Scotland, my theological training specialised in Church History, culminating in a doctorate based on research into the Scottish Reformation in Angus and the Mearns.[1] My first parish, Strathy and Halladale, was rich in history. Originally part of the ancient Parish of Farr, property of the earls and dukes of Sutherland, Strathy was created as a separate parish in the early eighteenth century explicitly as a result of the Highland Clearances – a new coastal parish for the crofters 'cleared' from Strath Naver, Strath Halladale and the rest of the hinterland.[2] Moving in 1993 to become Community Minister in Orkney, I came to live in a county rich in prehistoric sites and with its own unique blend of the Norse and Scottish traditions; a place which maintains a strong interest in its own history and traditions. Much of the remit of my post as first Community Minister in Orkney was directed, not so much towards the community as a whole, but rather more towards supporting the basic institutions of the Church of Scotland at parish and Presbytery level. Describing my remit at a meeting of other Community Ministers, I was asked with some surprise (even horror): 'But where does the Community come into it?' Seeking to contribute a Christian aspect to Orcadian history did in fact go some way to justifying the title of my post; it also brought me into contact and discussions with people and institutions beyond those of the Kirk and its office bearers.

This book, then, has a double focus. On the one hand, it builds on talks or papers produced when I was Community Minister for Orkney between 1993 and 1997 and adds to them, so that together they provide a narrative spanning the whole history so far of the Christian Church in Orkney. On the other, I try to place the historical chapters in the context of Orkney at the end of the twentieth century, the context in which I came to write them as a minister of the Church of Scotland. As it happened, the order in which things arose means that a choice has had to be made. The chapters could either follow the sequence in which my attention was drawn to aspects of Orkney's history, or they could follow the chronological pattern in which the Celtic Church was followed by the Norse invasions and the Secession came after the Reformation. For clarity I have chosen the latter; but nevertheless this book is not just a history, in the sense of looking objectively at the past and leaving it there. I believe that as Christians we are to learn from the past – from both successes and failures – and that we can use the past to help us understand our own problems and situation. Church History is the history of how people have put their faith into practice – and putting faith into practice is what the Church needs to do today.

Four years is a short time to spend in any county. I am very conscious that Orcadians often criticise 'incomers' who arrive and treat everyone before them as basically ignorant. I have learnt much of what is written here from previous writers about Orkney – hence the somewhat formal endnotes, which acknowledge my teachers. Nevertheless, I hope that those enthusiastic about Orkney's history will find something new here, besides my way of retelling an old story. Much has been written in the last few years on the earliest history of Orkney and Scotland that previous authors did not have available; and, besides, I have tried to incorporate a theological perspective not normally suitable in history. In further justification, I may say that I was originally *invited* to give the talks on which this book is based!

The book is dedicated to the members and congregations of the Church of Scotland in Orkney, with thanks; and also to Rev. Prof. Alec Cheyne who at New College, Edinburgh, first introduced me to the world of Scottish Church History and later encouraged me to spend time on research on the Scottish Reformation.

Rev. Dr Frank D. Bardgett
Secretary Depute: Department of National Mission, The Church of Scotland

North Queensferry, 2000.

---

1 Frank Bardgett, *Scotland Reformed: the Reformation in Angus and the Mearns* (John Donald, Edinburgh, 1989).
2 Frank Bardgett, *North Coast Parish* (Northern Printers, Thurso, 1990).

Chapter 1

The Mystery of the Prehistoric

Orkney has a wealth of prehistoric sites, of which Maes Howe and Skara Brae are simply the best known.[1] The homestead now called Knap of Howar on the island of Papa Westray claims to be the oldest known house in Europe: dated at c.3800 BC, it was thus inhabited the best part of six thousand years ago. The great ring of standing stones at Brodgar, standing in the midst of a landscape rich in burial mounds, ancient villages and single stones, is described by some as 'the heart of Orkney'. It is possible for the tourist to spend a week wholly engaged in exploring the variety of ancient tombs in the care of Historic Scotland, learning to distinguish between the different styles of building c.3000 BC.[2]

These dates are difficult to understand. We read them, but they don't grip the imagination. One modern historian of Scotland, T. C. Smout, suggested that the daily life of the Scottish people c.AD 1830, though in modern times, was as remote from the late twentieth century experience as the worlds of 'the Druids, the Natchez and the Tartars'.[3] Professor Smout asked: 'Who now knows what it was like to be fed only upon three meals of potatoes a day?' If a mental jump of only 170 years is too great, how shall we cope with a gap of three, four, five or six thousand years? How can we know what it was like to live in Orkney and work in the shadow of the Ring of Brodgar when it was one of the largest operational public structures in northern Europe? We find the time of the Viking Earls of Orkney fascinating and remote – their language and social structure a remnant memory – and they flourished a thousand years ago. The first Christians and Jesus himself are a mere two thousand years ago compared to the four and five thousand year old tombs and houses.

Try taking a piece of string. Tie one end down – that end represents the present. Tie a knot every foot to mark every hundred years going back into the past. Events like the French Revolution (1789) are very recent – even if they are mental and social worlds away from us today. Foot by foot go back, if you have room! – a thousand years – two thousand – five thousand. For all these years, Orkney has been continuously inhabited. Generations have been born, had children, worked and died. Their language has changed several times. Different waves of incomers have come and gone and stayed. The islands have been governed at different times by different political groups and nations. Nevertheless the string of time has been continuous – a succession of peoples as well as of events. We are connected by the string to all who came before us: they and us, part of one story.

Go back before 3000 BC. The vast sheets of ice of the last Ice Age are thought to have abandoned Scotland *c.*10000 BC. Scientists call the four thousand years between the melting of the ice and the coming of farmers the *mesolithic period*. During this period, which itself lasted

Standing Stone, Stoneyhill, Harray

twice as long as the time that separates us from New Testament times, hunters and their families came north, following the herds that were their prey and life, as the herds moved into the new lands. Archaeologists have discovered sites from this period in Orkney dating human occupation of these islands, even if at first by these transient people, back some 8500 years. Some specialists also speculate that people may well have been here before the ice – back into the *palaeolithic period*. Certainly there is evidence of human sites in southern Britain from 35000 years ago, lasting to the coming of the ice sheets after 25000 before present. Fifteen thousand years of ice, however, would have destroyed any trace those early peoples might have left in these islands.[4] Such expanses of time make the whole modern history of European civilisation – of Christendom – seem merely the last few minutes of an already long year. Your room would probably not be large enough for such a length of string!

So people lived and farmed these islands five thousand years ago.[5] Generations later, others dug the ditch around Brodgar with sweat and – no doubt – complaints. They looked for the course of the sun along the hills of Hoy as the year progressed. We are told that they lived by farming and fishing. Their world included dogs and sheep, pigs and goats, cod and birds' eggs. They made decorative items to wear, carefully designed and built homes, and were (on the whole) dead before they reached the age of thirty.[6] We are also told they expended colossal

The Stone of Setter, Eday

amounts of energy and time in building their monuments and tombs of stone: thousands of man-hours for each tomb, for Maes Howe even a hundred thousand man-hours, and each hour more precious, a higher percentage of a lifetime's work, than we can imagine.

These were people like us: people who spoke and thought and planned and tried to interpret the universe and their experience of life; people who changed the world around them, building with such effort and determination that no generation in Orkney ever since has surpassed their greatest works.

Of course, there are aspects of their lifestyle that we cannot understand. Why, of all their works, was it the tombs that were of such great importance that they have survived the millennia? Were they so frightened by the dead that they sought to lock them away in tombs of stone? Or did they so honour their ancestors that they built them homes to last for ever? What was the great stone ring for – a place for meetings and deciding: the equivalent of the Council Offices? A place for worship and ceremony – like St Magnus Cathedral? A place for exploring the relationships of the heavens – an Observatory? Or all of these combined – or something totally different? The single stones stand on hills and ridges, or in relation to each other, in locations that to this day appear to convey meaning – but their 'language' is totally untranslatable. My feeling is that those who built them had a sense of space – for land and water and sky; that in this sense of space, in their concern for the dead, they sought to understand the spiritual meaning of the universe and their place within it. Time has destroyed the key to unlock the symbols of their faith – perhaps the key was deliberately thrown away. The monuments remain enigmas.

The Christian Gospel is proclaimed as a faith for all – what, then, of the generations who lived before Jesus? Jesus, this new-comer and late-comer in historic time? We so easily assume that the world as we know it began with the coming of the written histories in Greek and Latin, unquestioningly accepting a western-orientated filter that screens out all history before Julius Caesar and all peoples beyond the bounds of Europe and the Mediterranean. We so easily assume that all that really matters are the last two millennia 'In the Year of Our Lord'. But people like us lived in Orkney three thousand years before Jesus was born – a thousand years longer than have passed since his death. What has the salvation offered in his Name to do with them? What sort of relationship did they have with our God, whom we worship as Father, Son and Holy Spirit, the eternal Three and One, and whose Name and Nature were then unknown because they had yet to be revealed?

It is easy to dismiss this question as speculation. What matters, we might think, is our own relationship with Jesus; it is folly and presumption to guess what we are not told. I accept that there is some truth in this: what does indeed matter first is our own relationship to Christ. But the question posed by the ancient monuments of Orkney is not just obscure theological speculation: it helps us to think about the character of the God we worship. For is the Christian God really a tribal God for Europe and its former colonies? Is and was the full salvation offered in Jesus only available to those cultures to whom his history has been brought, and to those peoples who were fortunate to live in the last minutes of world history 'AD'? Or has our God opened His Kingdom to all – *all*, throughout time from the dawning until now? So what can be said by the Christian Faith to the prehistoric people of Orkney?

There are texts in the New Testament that try to address this question.[7] Two Letters in the New Testament refer to the 'mystery' of the Gospel – referring to the fact that the Good News of Jesus had indeed been hidden from previous generations but was now disclosed. Paul, particularly, had a personal interest in the relationship of his own people, the Jews, and their ancient traditions of faith and worship, to the revelation in Jesus. That doctrine especially connected with him, salvation by faith, was worked out as he struggled with this historical question. Paul concluded that salvation for either Jew or Gentile, whether before or after Jesus, whether before or after Moses, had been by faith. That is the argument of the Letter to the Galatians, of the Letter to the Romans. The faith Paul wrote of was an attitude of mind and heart, reliant on God, trusting and seeking Him as far as He was known, so that the salvation of God was open to all who had (according to the light of their time) this faith.

The manner of exercising faith in God open to Orcadians five thousand years ago is no longer open to us: the mystery hidden from them has, of course, been disclosed to us. Nevertheless, I believe that it is not inappropriate to think of these ancient peoples as having a part in the Kingdom of our God. For me, this New Testament emphasis that God's Kingdom was, is, and always has been open to people of faith is central to what we know about God: that He is, and always has been, loving towards all He has made – no matter what period or culture or nation they belong to in the sweep of history. Ultimately, the Good News of Jesus is that our welcome by God is assured by him, and received by us in trust and commitment. The ways in which we express our faith are secondary and of less importance.

These musings about prehistory are relevant to more than the history of Orkney. During my time in Orkney, the islands' weekly newspaper, *The Orcadian*, printed letters asserting that the Orcadian way of life was threatened by incomers. Accusations of 'racism' were sometimes murmured across both sides of the Orkney-born and incomer divide. It is a fact that the population of Orkney increased by 15 per cent between 1971 and 1991, and continues to grow by immigration.[8] At the same time, folk are moving house away from the North Isles, to be closer to the centre of things in Kirkwall. Very substantial social changes lie behind the accusations that something of importance to older generations appears to be being lost or destroyed.

Meantime, the Church of Scotland's Orkney congregations continue to welcome as new members those from other denominations who, on moving north, want to worship with us. They bring experience of different styles of worship, different expectations; sometimes they are slow to understand the strength of feeling behind Orkney's older forms. The ministers themselves are 'from south', and have been trained by a denomination whose Articles commit it to 'seek and promote union with other Churches'.[9] Some members, Orkney-born, may feel that 'their' church is being changed by the insensitive. Others, from south, may feel that our congregations are less receptive, less spiritual, less progressive than they might be. It is surely relevant, then, that our welcome by God depends on faith – and on faith alone, and not on our loyalty to particular variants of the Christian traditions of worship, or on which building we happen to find convenient for worship, or on where and when we were born.

Paul's prayer, the practical corollary of the doctrine of justification by faith, still has its challenge:

May the God who gives endurance and encouragement give you a spirit of unity among yourselves as you follow Christ Jesus, so that with one heart and mouth you may glorify the God and Father of our Lord Jesus Christ. Accept one another, then, just as Christ accepted you, in order to bring praise to God. *(Romans 15:5-7)*

1   Before taking up my post in Orkney, I was told: 'You'll get asked to speak to a lot of Woman's Guilds' and that was right! In just over three years, I reached a tally into double figures for talks to Guild branches, sometimes by myself and sometimes accompanying a musical contribution by my wife Alison. One early request, for a talk of my own choice, came from St Andrew's Guild. So on 12 July 1994, I took along a ball of string, a series of postcards and a collection of clothes pegs to speak about 'Orkney's Prehistory and Christian Faith'. The topic stayed in my mind, and I contributed an expanded version of the talk to an Open Evening arranged by the Presbytery's Education Committee on 5 December the same year. 'Talks', however, were what these were. I wasn't asked to lecture – so I didn't have a full or even a partial script. Rather, it was a case of taking things to talk about, on a declared theme – much as someone showing slides speaks 'off the cuff' to the prearranged programme as each new picture is shown. This chapter is therefore a reconstruction, without the advantage of a large room across which to hang my ball of string.
2   Anna Ritchie, *Exploring Scotland's Heritage – Orkney* (The Stationery Office, Edinburgh, 1996).
3   T.C. Smout, *A Century of the Scottish People* (London, 1986) p.1.
4   C.R. Wickham-Jones, *Scotland's First Settlers* (Historic Scotland/B.T. Batsford Ltd, London, 1994).
5   P.J. Ashmore, *Neolithic and Bronze Age Scotland* (Historic Scotland/B.T. Batsford Ltd, London, 1996) p.45.
6   Anna Ritchie, *Prehistoric Orkney* (Historic Scotland/B.T. Batsford Ltd, 1995) p.61.
7   Ephesians 3:5,9; Colossians 1:25,26; Romans 2:7-11 and 14-15; Hebrews 11:1-2; Acts 17:30-1.
8   *Community Care Plan* (Orkney Islands Council/Orkney Health Board, Kirkwall, 1997).
9   ed. James L. Weatherhead, *The Constitution and Laws of the Church of Scotland* (The Board of Practice and Procedure, Edinburgh, 1997) p.160.

Chapter 2

The Celtic Missionaries: breadth and depth to the mystery

During 1997, all Scottish Churches were invited to join a celebration of faith based on the anniversaries of the early saints Ninian and Columba.[1] This was, in turn, part of an ecumenical celebration throughout England, Scotland and Ireland. The English churches were remembering the arrival of Augustine at Canterbury. The then President of Ireland, Mary Robinson, attended events in Scotland celebrating links of faith between these countries, whose national institutions have recently been predominantly Catholic and Protestant. 'The Celtic Cross is a sign of love uniting Scotland and the Christian Faith. In 1997 Scotland remembers the first mission to Whithorn in 397, the work of

Symbol for the Scottish Churches' 'Year of Faith', 1997

Ninian, and the life of Columba who died in 597.'[2]

Materials circulated by, among others, the Church of Scotland's Department of National Mission, invited Presbyteries to:

- Plan an event at local or regional level celebrating and explaining the Christian Faith in the light of the Celtic heritage. You could mount a display or exhibition, have music and drama, involve artists and reach out into the local community.
- Consider a missionary initiative which responds to the achievements of Ninian, Columba and other missionaries in evangelism, social care and environmental concern.
- Explore the roots of Christianity in your area and the routes by which the Gospel travels linking you with other churches and countries.
- Undertake a new development in the worship and prayer life of your community.
- Remember that the vision of Ninian and Columba belongs to all Scottish Christians, so why not plan together with other churches and groups.

Initially, the question was whether the people of Orkney, with its strong ties to the Norse east and not the Gaelic west, would really wish to take an interest in these events. Old Orcadian tradition, however, did in fact link the Celtic missions to the islands. The Orkney poet and storyteller, George Mackay Brown, wrote that:[3]

> The mystery of light out of darkness has been with us since the builders of Maeshowe five thousand years ago. The Celtic missionaries give the mystery breadth and depth.

Before the sixth century: from the time of Christ to AD 500

Little is known for sure of Orkney's history in the early centuries of the Christian era. Immediately before the Viking period the islands formed part of the realm of the Picts, a Celtic people, and, being good farmland, had by then been inhabited for several millennia by sizeable communities.

The Christian faith had come to the British Isles by the second century after Christ, during Roman rule in what was to become England. The Faith spread across the Imperial borders to Ireland and also north of

Hadrian's Wall. After the withdrawal of the Empire from its British Province c. AD 410 and lacking any other central authority, the churches of the Celtic peoples (though remaining Catholic in terms of basic doctrine) developed their own forms of worship and organisation, especially in Ireland.

The Roman Empire had enabled western Europe within its boundaries to develop a culture based on cities, from York in the west to beyond Jerusalem in the east. Once the Empire adopted the Christian Faith, these cities became the basic units of the church, each with its own bishop. The non-Roman Celtic peoples, however, retained a much more flexible social pattern, based on tribes and family units. Moreover, they remained pagan for centuries after the Emperor Constantine accepted Christianity in AD 313. Celtic Christianity,[4] therefore, although it knew of bishops, placed a greater emphasis on monasticism; seeking places where Christians, both men and women, could create new Christian 'families', set apart from an often hostile world, to put their faith into practice under the paternal discipline of an Abbot.

Living on and trading across the borders of the Empire, the Celts were able to obtain and exchange Christian texts and ideas from lands that had seen the origins of the Faith, using these eastern resources and adapting them to their own culture; expressing them in their own art-forms. Whereas the devout in the east went into the desert to test their faith and make space for prayer, the Irish sought solitude in the islands and oceans to the north. Whereas the Romans built their cities and their churches massively out of enduring stone, the more mobile Celts were content to worship out of doors, their spirituality at home in the transitory world of nature.

The sixth and seventh centuries – the Celtic church of the Scots

The Faith seems to have spread to the southern Picts by the late fifth or early sixth century, perhaps associated with the work of Ninian, bishop at Whithorn.[5] Some decades later, Irish Celtic Christianity came with Columba and the Scots to Iona; Columba died in AD 597 having also made contact with the northern Picts. During Columba's lifetime, the people of what is now northern Scotland and the Northern Isles seem to have remained hostile to the Christian faith, though Scottish Celtic monks of the family of Iona, ascetics and explorers, reached as far north across the seas as Iceland. Meeting King Bridei mac Maelchon at his court somewhere near modern Inverness, Columba asked for assurances that Iona's wandering monks would be protected if they came to Orkney:[6]

> Some of our people have gone forth seeking a remote place across the unsailed seas; should they, after long travel, reach the islands of Orkney, command this king, whose hostages you hold, that no evil befall them within his territory.

From the evidence of Columba's biographer Adomnán, we get the name of the first Christian *known* (what others are now unknown?) to have reached Orkney: Cormac, an Iona monk for whose safety Columba was concerned.[7] The monastic voyager Brendan is also linked with journeys to and beyond the Northern Isles before AD 600. Possibly some of their followers settled in Orkney whether permanently or just for periods of retreat to temporary hermitages, while the seas were open during the summer. 'Stack-sites', the remains of small buildings on the peaks of rock stacks off the coast, do exist, for example off Hoy, Stronsay and Westray. Some have identified these as Celtic hermitage or monastic sites, but archaeologists can offer no positive evidence for this.[8]

These early voyages were not primarily missions – their first motive was not to convert the residents of the north; rather, the voyagers were seeking solitude for prayer and spiritual struggle, deliberately casting themselves adrift as pilgrims upon the oceans of God. 'Retreat', however, is hardly an appropriate word to describe these voyages – dangerous, arduous, testing. 'Engagement' was what they were about, engagement with the hostile elements, sometimes with hostile populations; knowing the God whom they described as 'the monk-prover' was Lord of all of creation, and to be trusted even to and beyond the rim of the world.

> ... he crossed the long-haired sea.
> He crossed the wave-strewn wild region,
> foam-flecked, seal-filled,
> savage, bounding, seething, white-tipped,
> pleasing, doleful. [9]

This mode of practising the faith – strange and even alien as it seems to us today – must nevertheless have brought Christianity to the attention of the native peoples of Orkney. We have no idea what they thought of it – beyond Columba's suspicions that their reactions might be hostile.

The era of these voyages did not end until the coming of the Norse drove the monks from their summer hermitages. The monk and author Dicuil, who fled from Iona and had settled at the court of Charlemagne by 814, reported the stories of fellow monastics who had been driven from Iceland by Vikings about 795. Dicuil's writings show knowledge of the longer daylight hours of the far north, of the arctic ice-pack, of native sheep and seafowl. They show, too, that contacts between the Scottish monasteries of the west and the Northern Isles continued, despite the changing church allegiances of the ruling houses of the Picts, until the Norse conquest.[10]

During the hundred years after 600, the powerful holiness of Columba and the monastic zeal of his followers spread the Faith from Iona beyond the Scottish kingdom of Dal Riata into the lands of the Picts. By the time Columba's biographer, Adomnán, was Abbot of Iona in the 680s, the Pictish Kingdom had become Christian. Iona, it must be said, was one of the greatest monastic centres of Europe: for learning, for art, for collections of Christian texts; a centre of the devout and the committed. It, too, was in touch with other such centres, both in Ireland and in continental Europe. Its traditions were those of the family of Columba, maintained with some pride against the growing authority of the Holy Father who was Bishop of Rome – where the date of Easter was calculated by a different formula, and authority in the church centred around Bishops rather than Abbots.[11]

In the Tankerness House Museum, Kirkwall, are collections of Pictish stone crosses and of cross-headed pins; and the remains of a Celtic ecclesiastical bell – physical evidence that the Christian Faith in its Celtic form was present in Orkney (? c.600 – 800).[12] These remains, with others now held elsewhere,[13] demonstrate a family likeness with similar finds in the Pictish lands around the Moray Firth and in modern Angus.[14] Regretfully, we cannot claim 'ownership' of any of the extant documentary treasures of the Celtic Church – the great illustrated Gospels with their intricate, decorated pages.

Illustration based on an early Christian altar cross, Flotta

8th century Christian cross-slab found in the St Boniface Kirkyard, Papa Westray [courtesy of Tankerness House Museum, Kirkwall]

Early Christian incised stone found on the Brough of Birsay [courtesy of Tankerness House Museum, Kirkwall]

Early Christian incised cross, Broch of Burrian, North Ronaldsay [from a 19th century photograph]

The eighth century church of the Picts

Though they increasingly shared a common Celtic spirituality, Picts and Scots were political rivals. Nechtan, King of Picts (died AD 732) aligned the Church in Pictland with Rome. He supported the authority of Curitán, who came from the influential monastery at Wearmouth[15] in Northumbria to become Bishop of Ross and probably took the name of Boniface.[16] Those of the Iona family (unlike their abbot, Adomnán) unwilling to conform to Roman customs, were expelled west of the spine of Britain. In his *History of the English Church and People* (completed 731) the Northumbrian monk Bede copied in full a tract written by his own Abbot Ceolfrid of Wearmouth to King Nechtan arguing for the rightness of the Catholic practice of Rome.[17] The cult of Peter was deliberately spread to counteract the Scottish Columban-centred Church. By thus associating the Pictish Kingdom with the Europe-wide catholicity of Rome, Nechtan sought to marginalise the Scots just as he sought to isolate them with his alliance with Northumbria.

The distinctive Celtic artistic expressions of spirituality no doubt continued to influence the Orkney church, and the voyaging monks must have maintained some contacts. The Church in Northumbria, though it conformed to Rome after 664 and came under the authority of the archdiocese of York, had its bishops based at a monastic church at Hexham and at its own island of monks, Lindisfarne, itself founded from Iona *c.*630. Nevertheless beyond the technical details – the shape of the clerical tonsure and the date of the celebration of Easter – in retrospect important differences between the Scottish and the Roman disciplines may be emphasised. Whereas Iona valued its own local traditions (and hence accepted the validity of the local traditions of others too), Rome sought an ideal of uniformity throughout western Christendom, from which separate regional traditions came later to be described as heresy. With this insistence came a degree of status, authority and power conferred upon the various ranks of the priesthood as the vicars of Peter, the anointed interpreters of the apostolic tradition. Authority in the Celtic church appears to have been more charismatic and personal, honouring a self-effacing humility that shrank from the trappings and symbols of power. Moreover, Rome smiled on monasticism according to the rule of Benedict. Benedict expected stability of his monks, turning his face against the Irish-Celtic urge to pilgrimage upon the oceans, and requiring his followers to live and stay in fixed communities. The joint foundation at Wearmouth/Jarrow was Benedictine from its origin in the 670s; Iona was refounded under the Rule of Benedict *c.*1204.

Dr Raymond Lamb, formerly archaeologist of the Orkney Heritage Society, suggests the following thesis:[18]

- Orkney became part of the Kingdom of the Picts 'early in the eighth century'.
- Royal authority endowed Christian clergy and buildings with estates in the islands creating 'a highly organised ecclesiastical power structure throughout the country'.
- These clergy were known to the later Norse as the 'Papar'.
- The historic placenames 'Papa' – seven in Orkney – were associated with them.
- Several Churches were dedicated to St Peter and are still associated with major brochs.
- The seat of the 'diocese' was Papa Westray, where the ancient church of St Boniface stands on a site dating back to the eighth century.

If this thesis is correct, then Orkney's institutional church by the eighth century owed more to Roman patterns of episcopal organisation than to Columba's monastic family. Priests enjoyed royal patronage and high status, and were granted valuable lands to sustain their church. One in Shetland was depicted in stone on horseback, an emphatic assertion of authority. They held such sway that their lands and islands still bear the name of the 'Papar' to this day. Orkney would thus conform to the pattern of much of northern Europe, where Christianity came from the top downwards, the religion of ambitious kings and their warrior-followers, imposing order and stability within a culture based on gift-exchange. Some question whether such a version of Christianity deserves to be entitled 'faith'. Professor Gordon Donaldson identified the four most common elements leading to baptism in the era of 'conversion' – 'marriage, miracles, conquest and compulsion'. None of these appear to the contemporary Christian to have much to do with the Jesus of the New Testament. Professor Donaldson concluded that Christianity could hardly be said to have permeated society as a whole in the Celtic period.[19]

Even if Orkney's eighth century Pictish Church came under the authority of a missionary bishop, this does not, of course, exclude the possibility of there being monastic settlements from this period in the islands. Unfortunately it is almost impossible for archaeologists to differentiate between monastic and ordinary farming communities in this period. Anna Ritchie, in her 1996 survey of Orkney's ancient monuments, accepted that part of the major settlement around St Boniface, Papa Westray, was monastic. She further suggested that the small Norse monastery on Eynhallow might have had Celtic origins.[20] Professor Christopher Morris, who excavated the Chapel on the Brough of Deerness, uncovered traces of a pre-Norse timber Chapel – but was unable to identify the sort of community that it served.[21] Monasticism was an important part of church life in both the Roman and Columban traditions; it would be surprising if Orkney had known nothing of the discipline.

Control by the Pictish realm may not have been beneficial to Orkney. The Annals record Pictish warlords raiding and devastating Orkney: King Aed *c.*580, King Bridei in 681, perhaps from Burghead, perhaps from the Golspie area.[22] Certainly the eighth century pattern of churches is Pictish, but Orkney's Crosses are small and fragmentary compared to the elaborate and expensive Pictish Crosses of Angus and Ross-shire and Sutherland. Archaeologists suggest that there was a widespread 'decline and contraction of the community' in Orkney, beginning in the seventh century and continuing to the Norse period. Long-established settlements grew smaller, with more rubbish and rubble evident. Was this the result, too, of subjugation by the Pictish Kings? Did it make the Norse conquest easier? From whom were the *Papar*'s estates taken – lands Dr Lamb describes as 'prime-quality farmland'? Did Bridei or his successors confiscate the lands of their Orcadian opponents and use their estates to endow their Roman form of Church? If the Church, though wealthy, was associated with a repressive, southern, regime, how did this affect Orcadian understanding of the Faith?[23]

In his history *The Rise of Western Christendom*, Peter Brown writes of Northern Europe:[24]

> Local warriors gave support to the Church in exchange for the impressive counter-gift of blessing in this world and salvation in the next . . . Christianity spread, if at all, at ground level. It radiated outwards from scattered centres, through intermittent, highly charged contact with the sacred: through high moments of festival, through pilgrimage to high places, through memorable supernatural duels between Christian holy persons and their visible and invisible enemies – sorcerers, demons, fire and the bleak hostility of the northern weather.

Professor Brown's qualification 'if at all' is worth noting. The language of faith was Latin; the practice of the Christian religion was centred on 'the religious' – priests and monks. The institutional Church was here; how far the Faith had touched the ordinary folk of Orkney before the coming of the Norse is almost impossible to estimate. In Northumbria, where a wealth of carved crosses, early churches and illuminated manuscripts survive from the rich Christian culture of the seventh century, it was necessary to prescribe a table of appropriate penances for baptised Christians who practised pagan divination, sacrificed to demons or used pagan spells to heal the sick. In Orkney, with its wealth of prehistoric standing stones and tombs, the very scenery must have echoed with the older faiths. The Stones of Stenness still had some ritual use as late as the sixth century.[25] Even though the island may be seen as convenient to both the Orkney and the Shetland groups, was there something marginal about a creed whose eighth-century centre was Papa Westray? Archaeologists place St Boniface Kirk on the site of a major broch and settlement, now vanished. Was Pictish royal power maintained in Orkney from bases like Papay and the Brough of Birsay, dependent on the sea?

It would, of course, be pleasant to think that the influence of the peaceful and prayerful earlier voyagers also survived: several church or chapel sites have ancient dedications to St Colm, otherwise St Columba. Archaeological Surveys list:

- St Columba's Parish Church (later known as Burness), Sanday

- St Colm's Chapel, Sanday
- St Colm's Kirk, Rousay
- St Colm's Chapel, Kirk Hope, South Walls

The ancient church on the Brough of Birsay has also known a dedication to St Colm, though evidence for this is relatively modern. Such dedications as these, together with the surviving Celtic crosses, are given by Rev. J. Craven, Episcopal priest in Kirkwall at the turn of the century, as evidence of 'missions' to Orkney, first by the generation of Ninian and then by Ionan monks led by Cormac. He pictures Cormac attempting the short sea crossing of the Pentland Firth and landing at Burwick, South Ronaldsay; and suggests that the former Chapel to St Columba, near the site of St Mary's Church there, may recall 'the first foundation of the Iona brotherhood in Orkney'. All of this, however, is most uncertain and a sixth century origin of the dedication unproveable. The Christian Norse adopted Columba as one of their saints once they had settled in the Hebrides and the Northern Isles, and all of these dedications may therefore be eleventh and twelfth century products of the Church of the Norse Earldom, local alternatives to the cult of St Magnus and survivals neither from the eighth century Pictish Church nor from the even earlier sixth or seventh century monastic voyagers.

> According to the *Hákonar Saga*, when Alexander II of Scotland was lying in the sound off Kerrera Island in Argyll in 1249 on his way to attack King Hakon's fleet in the Hebrides, the Scottish monarch saw Columba in a dream. Of enormous stature and repulsive appearance, he appeared in the company of Olaf the saint of Norway and St Magnus of Orkney. Columba in Norse imagination had taken on something of the awful and sinister qualities associated in Viking times with visions of the war god, Odin.[26]

It has been said of the Chapel on the Brough of Deerness[27] that it gives a good impression of the age of the first missionaries. It may be that the ancient tradition of the Brough as a consecrated place does indeed come from the monk-voyagers. Those of the Iona tradition do seem to have looked to island sites partially isolated from nearby secular influence. Archaeological investigations, however, can do no more than state that a timber Chapel preceded the Norse stone version whose remains we now enjoy.[28]

Further, examination of the 997 connection with St Ninian also causes reconsideration of an alternative picture of the first Christian links to Orkney. In 1956 the Church of Scotland Evangelist D.P. Thomson wrote in his booklet *Orkney through the Centuries – Lights and Shadows of the Church's life in the Northern Isles*:[29]

> ... the Christian Gospel owes its origin in Orkney to the mission inaugurated by Ninian, the apostle to the Picts, at Whithorn, in Galloway, in the year 397 AD. If that great evangelist and missionary did not himself penetrate as far north as Orkney and Shetland his immediate followers certainly did, and they carried their master's name and reputation, his fame and message and distinctive tradition, with them there, as they did wherever they went. What Christianity has meant to these islands through the centuries dates back unquestionably to this heroic pioneer.

D.P. Thomson cited Dr Frank Knight as one of those who believed that the pioneer evangelist Ninian came himself to Orkney.

The Chapel on the Brough of Deerness

'Ninian's enthusiasm as a messenger of Christ', he writes, 'carried him even over the stormy Pentland Firth to Orkney. The island at South Ronaldsay had a chapel at Stow's Head which bore his name, and on the neighbouring mainland, in St Andrew's Parish, another chapel preserved the memory of his visit. The extremest north island of the Orkneys is called North Ronaldsay, but the Sagas always style it Ronansay – St Ninian's Isle. It was the name by which it was known in the ninth century when the Norsemen appeared.' . . . It was here in 1870 that Dr William Traill, the proprietor of the island, discovered in North Ronaldsay the inscribed slab known as 'The Broch of Burrian's Cross' – unmistakably of the same type as those associated with Ninian's famous monastery and missionary centre in Galloway, at which all his evangelists were trained. On that site also was found a bell of the Niniantic period.

The foreword to D.P. Thomson's booklet expresses the evangelist's thanks and debt to Rev. Harald Mooney, former minister of Deerness. No doubt the booklet can be taken as expressing the opinions of Mr Mooney, whose parish church's dedication to St Ninian is no older than 1931 – from the occasions of a church union and the temporary stranding of SS *St Ninian* on a sandbank off the Deerness coast.[30] 'D.P.' had been visiting Orkney as part of the 'Tell Scotland' mission of those years; folk still in the kirk today remember attending his meetings – he would have had little time for personal historical research.

But were D.P. Thomson and Dr Knight correct in linking Ninian with Orkney? A modern historian writes about Bishop Ninian of Whithorn:[31]

> Ninian was born of British parents some time in the late 5th century and educated in a Christian centre in southern Scotland. Early in his career, perhaps in the early years of the sixth century, he travelled through Gaul and Italy to Rome, now a revived centre of learning and home to a newly prestigious papacy . . . On his return to north Britain, he was consecrated a missionary bishop to the Picts, and established a number of churches and cemeteries between the Forth and the Mounth . . . Towards the end of his life, perhaps around the mid sixth century, Ninian returned to Whithorn, rebuilt the Church there and dedicated it to Saint Martin, and it was there that he died and was buried (before 563).

If Dr Macquarrie is right, then AD 397 as the traditional date of Ninian at Whithorn is certainly wrong; so too was the '97 connection as the reason for remembering him that year; and so too is the myth that he was the founding saint of the Orkney Church. It seems more likely that, at the time that the eighth century Pictish Church was seeking to distinguish itself from the Scots and Iona, they may well have named places after the Picts' apostle Ninian – so that the Ninian names in both Shetland and Orkney could be contemporary with those to Boniface on Papa Westray and to the various dedications to St Peter.

And so for my choice of 'first known Christian' I turn to Cormac, the contemporary of Columba. Cormac, too, has a connection in legend with Deerness. Edwin Muir wrote in his Autobiography:

> My mother's name was Elizabeth Cormack, and my knowledge of her family again goes back only to her father, Edwin Cormack, after whom I was named. There is in Deerness a ruined chapel which was built in the eighth or ninth century by an Irish priest called Cormack the Sailor, who was later canonised; it is only a few miles from Haco, the farm where my mother was born. Whether the names are connected over that great stretch of time in that small corner no one can say; but it is conceivable, for in Orkney families have lived in the same place for many hundreds of years, and I like to think that some people in the parish, myself among them, may have a saint among their ancestors.

It is to Cormac and the monk-voyagers that I look if asked for the relevance of all this to today's church. These were men who set sail northwards, looking for a 'desert in the ocean' for prayer, testing their faith on the oceans of God. These monks sailed in the faith that wherever they went, they could not go beyond the realm and rule of Christ. Their world must often have seemed dark and dangerous; in their small ships they were tremendously exposed to the elements. Yet they first made the paths in the northern seas that the Vikings and the European explorers subsequently followed to the New World. Our modern secular and cynical society often seems equally hostile to those who believe the Christian faith. We can learn something from the courage, the optimism, the prayerful venturing of those early Celtic monk-voyagers who first brought the faith to Orkney. And, just perhaps, Cormac himself did over-summer on the Brough of Deerness and founded a chapel there as a place of prayer!

The lasting icon for Celtic Christianity in Orkney is the intricate, unending knot that is featured on their stone work and of which the best local example is the Flotta Cross. Untying such a knot is impossible – it is there, before our eyes, but it has no ends to get hold of. Monastic voyagers certainly reached Orkney. The Pictish Church was certainly present in Orkney; but try too hard to pin it down to precise dates or sites or names, and it slips away back into the mists of eternity.

Celtic spirituality

Celtic society placed emphasis on the warrior and the war-band – on kingship and the family. Monks therefore left the world to become the warriors of Christ, their oath being given to him. In exchange, their Lord extended to them his protection in both this world and the next – and against enemies both human and demonic. The Celtic peoples lived in a world where the natural interlined with the supernatural; where spirits lived in wells and in forests; where trees and hills and water had

Pictish symbol stone
[courtesy of Tankerness House Museum, Kirkwall]

their own sacredness. As Christian imagery and doctrine gripped their minds, elements of the older mindset survived, reinterpreted, as part of a complex spirituality – centred on Christ, and delighting in his living world. Even in translation, the poetry of the church of the Dark Ages still has power today.

> Alone with none but thee, my God;
> I journey on my way;
> What need I fear, when thou art near,
> O King of night and day?
> More safe am I within thy hand,
> Than if a host did round me stand.
>
> My destined time is fixed by thee,
> And Death doth know his hour.
> Did warriors strong around me throng,
> They could not stay his power;
> No walls of stone can man defend
> When thou thy messenger dost send.
>
> The child of God can fear no ill,
> His chosen dread no foe;
> We leave our fate with thee, and wait
> Thy bidding when to go.
> 'Tis not from chance our comfort springs,
> Thou art our trust, O King of kings.
>
> *Attributed to St Columba*[32]

Further hymns originating with the Celtic Church can be found in the Church of Scotland third hymnbook. Hymn 402: *I bind unto myself today*, 'The breastplate of St Patrick', includes the verse:

> Christ be with me, Christ within me,
> Christ behind me, Christ before me,
> Christ beside me, Christ to win me,
> Christ to comfort and restore me,
> Christ beneath me, Christ above me,
> Christ in quiet, Christ in danger,

> Christ in hearts of all that love me,
> Christ in mouth of friend and stranger.

A recent version of this can also be found in *Songs of God's People* at # 19.[33]

In the hymnbook, number 401 *Today I arise* is also attributed to Patrick. Hymn 301 *Christ is the world's redeemer* is said to come from Columba. Hymn 87 *Be thou my vision* is simply said to be 'Ancient Irish' and includes:

> Be thou my battle-shield, sword for the fight;
> Be thou my dignity, thou my delight,
> Thou my soul's shelter, thou my high tower:
> Raise thou me heaven-ward, O Power of my power.

Writing about the Celtic Christianity of the early Irish and Hebridean peoples, Mary Low insists that it is important not to think first about buildings.[34] She believes that the present Abbey of Iona gives a wholly false picture of the Celtic past: its Benedictine predecessor being built 'to replace – or at best assimilate' the earlier Columban tradition. What churches or chapels were built, were not primarily for congregational use. The chapels on the Broughs of Birsay and Deerness could hardly contain many folk. Their main function was to shelter the altar and the clergy celebrating Mass – they were for 'the religious'. Ordinary life in the Dark Ages was conducted largely out of doors in the natural world. In many ways (and not the purely physical) it was less protected, more exposed than in our own day. Practising one's faith was not a matter of gathering 'held and protected by four strong walls' to concentrate on the inner world. The spirituality passed down by the ordinary folk of the Gaelic west contains a wealth of prayers for daily living: for sleeping and for kindling the household fire; for baptism and death; for driving cows and for milking; for fishing and rowing; for parting, for travelling; for justice, for protection.

This prayer, for night shielding, comes from Alexander Carmichael's nineteenth century collection of prayers and hymns from the Gaelic oral tradition.[35]

> My God and my Chief,
> I seek to Thee in the morning,
> My God and my Chief,
> I seek to Thee this night.
> I am giving Thee my mind,
> I am giving Thee my will,
> I am giving Thee my wish,
> My soul everlasting and my body.
> Mayest Thou be chieftain over me,
> Mayest Thou be master unto me,
> Mayest Thou be shepherd over me,
> Mayest Thou be guardian unto me,
> Mayest Thou be herdsman over me,
> Mayest Thou be guide unto me,
> Mayest Thou be with me, O Chief of Chiefs,
> Father Everlasting and God of the heavens.

This further extract from Carmichael's *Carmina Gadelica* is a blessing-prayer for one leaving on a journey.

> I set the keeping of Christ about thee,
> I send the guarding of God with thee,
> To possess thee, to protect thee
> From drowning, from danger, from loss,
> From drowning, from danger, from loss.
>
> The Gospel of the God of grace
> Be from thy summit to thy sole;
> The Gospel of Christ, King of salvation,
> Be as a mantle to thy body,
> Be as a mantle to thy body.
>
> Nor drowned be thou at sea,
> Nor slain be thou on land,
> Nor o'erborne be thou by man,
> Nor undone be thou by woman,
> Nor undone be thou by woman!

The distinction between magic charm and Christian prayer in this popular culture is none too clear: in later centuries the church's ministry frowned on the superstitions of both the Gaelic West and the Norse Northern Isles. Yet a sincere and Christian faith does shine from many of the verses valued by the Celtic peoples. Modern prayers composed in this tradition can be found in the Church of Scotland's new *Common Order*[36] under the index heading 'Celtic Prayers'. Indeed there is a flourishing modern publishing industry drawing from the Celtic traditions.

To sum up his research on Celtic Spirituality,[37] Dr Ian Bradley of Aberdeen's Theology Department looks to three key ideas: a theology that knew the presence of God within His world; a faith expressed in poetry and art; and pilgrimage as a leading expression of Christian commitment. Corresponding to these three 'ps' – presence, poetry and pilgrimage – he would have today's church learn three lessons from the Celtic period. Dr Bradley commends a *Celtic ministry of presence*, of being with, rather than always doing; *a way of mission* that comes over to the visual, imaginative and emotional areas of life and not just to the intellect; and *a sense that life is always in a state of change and movement* – that the chief aim of the church is neither to preserve but to transform the world, nor to preserve itself but to be transformed.

> To be a pilgrim was to take the outward path which acknowledged the reality of this inner journey of the individual human soul and to embark on a way which involved suffering, sacrifice and pain as well as consolations and companionship along the way and which ended, if indeed it ended at all, at the place of one's resurrection.

---

1 Orkney's participation in the 1997 celebration of the founding missions of the British churches took an appropriately varied number of forms. The parishes of Hoy and Walls, with their partner island Flotta, held a celebration that included, besides a special service, a visit from the Salvation Army Band and an evening social event. The parishes of Birsay, Harray and Sandwick organised a special Sunday evening service on the Brough of Birsay at the old Pictish/Norse Chapel there. The islands of Westray and Papa Westray put to this use their normal summer commemoration at the ancient Church of St Boniface on Papay. Sanday, North Ronaldsay and others used the theme in their own ways in Sunday worship. The Presbytery, through its

Education Committee, hosted a family event in Deerness on Saturday 7 June, to which some 250-300 people came, from various Mainland parishes and denominations, Shapinsay, and South Ronaldsay and Burray. The 'day' began with a barbecue at Dingieshowe ayre, provided by the summer outing of the charge of Evie, Firth and Rendall, to which was added ice cream when the summer picnic of Kirkwall's East Kirk arrived. Games were arranged on the beaches for the younger people; a 'Celtic missionary' (from Stromness) arrived on the beach with message, staff and bell. Coaches took away for a tour of Deerness those who preferred not to walk on what was a dry but fairly blustery afternoon. An Exhibition on the Celtic theme was arranged in the Deerness Community Hall, where the ladies of Deerness also provided teas and the Presbytery Resource Centre, a bookstall. A further group, including members of the Cathedral, walked to the ancient Chapel on the Brough of Deerness. Finally, we all gathered in St Ninian's Church, Deerness, for a late afternoon celebratory service. The Firth Praise Band (or part of it) helped lead enthusiastic praise and, with the help of young folk, we heard the story of Cormac, the first Christian known to have come to Orkney. It was a pick-and-mix day; some stayed throughout, some only came for the tea, or the games, or the walk. Some came in organised groups and some as individuals. The exhibition was subsequently borrowed by the Kirkwall Episcopal Church for its Sunday service. It has to be admitted that Deerness was chosen for this event partly because, as my home was in that parish, I thought its combination of beach, hall, Brough and Church were a suitable and usable combination.

2   From national publicity circulated by the Church of Scotland. The 397 date connection to Ninian is probably wrong – see below.
3   George Mackay Brown, *Winter Tales* (Flamingo, 1996) in the Foreword.
4   Some scholars think that the term 'Celtic Christianity' is flawed. The Celts were divided into many nations, in Britain and in Europe; no single church system united them. The faith of people like Columba was Christian in an orthodox sense, not different in fundamentals from that in non-Celtic lands; nor, in essentials, different from that followed in Rome. Some react against a 'romantic' picture of the Celts that panders to a late twentieth century 'New Age spirituality' consciously separate both from the practical traditions and ideals of the past and from the realities of modern Christian life. Some therefore prefer the term 'Columban Church' to stand for the tradition of monastic and community life that refers back to Columba as the leader and founder of a family of monasteries whose monks all looked to him. This title, too, has its problems. It ignores the role of Columba's predecessors and contemporaries as missionaries and founders of monasteries, just as Columba's biographer, Adomnán, ignored them. It suggests that the Columban pattern was the only pattern, whereas the Picts developed their own way of organising the church. Aware of the difficulties of the generalisation, I prefer to use 'Celtic Christianity' and try to avoid its pitfalls. For the 'Columban Church', see Ian Bradley, *Columba Pilgrim and Penitent 597-1997* (Glasgow, 1996) pp.64-7; for 'Celtic Christianity', see Ian Bradley, *The Celtic Way* (London, 1993) p.vii and throughout.

5 Alan Macquarrie, 'The date of Saint Ninian's Mission: a reappraisal' in *Records of the Scottish Church History Society* (vol xxiii pt.1, Edinburgh, 1987). Macquarrie convincingly 'moves' Ninian from the late Roman period *c*.397 to the 'first half of the sixth century'.
6 ed. William Reeves, *Life of St Columba by Adomnán* (1874 and other editions) p.104.
7 B.H. Hossack, *Kirkwall in the Orkneys* (Kirkwall 1900, reprinted 1986) p.1 refers to the mission, AD 431, of Palladius to the Scots and his supposed ordination of a missionary bishop for Orkney, citing David Calderwood, *History of the Kirk of Scotland* (Wodrow Society 1842-9), i p.40. Palladius' mission was to the Scots in Ireland, however; the reference to Orkney seems due to a misreading of placenames.
8 The brochures for tourists produced by the various island Community Councils do not echo the highly cautious professional descriptions of sites by Dr Raymond Lamb in *The Archaeological Sites and Monuments of Scotland*: 'Sanday and North Ronaldsay' (11), 'Rousay, Egilsay and Wyre' (16), 'Papa Westray and Westray' (19), 'Eday and Stronsay' (23), 'Shapinsay, St Andrews and Deerness' (27), 'Hoy and Waas' (29) (RCAHMS, Edinburgh, 1980, 1982, 1983, 1984, 1987, 1989).
9 From a poem about Columba attributed to Beccan mac Luigdech, cited in Ian Bradley, op.cit. (1996).
10 Alfred P. Smyth, *Warlords and Holy Men – Scotland AD 80-1000* (London, 1984) pp.166-73.
11 Anna Ritchie, *Iona* (Historic Scotland/B.T. Batsford, London, 1997) pp.63-4 and Alfred P. Smyth, op.cit. (1984) pp.75, 119.
12 The Saevar Howe/Saverough Bell, however, is placed by some archaeologists in a Norse context, where it might be considered loot from anywhere! Anna Ritchie, 'Birsay around AD 800' in *Orkney Heritage* vol. 2 (Kirkwall, 1983).
13 Rev. J.B. Craven, *History of the Church in Orkney* vol. i (Kirkwall, 1900) contains illustrations of several early cross-slabs, some of which are reproduced here.
14 Sally M. Foster, *Picts, Gaels and Scots* (Historic Scotland/B.T. Batsford, London, 1997) p.67.
15 Wearmouth, dedicated to St Peter, originated in a joint foundation with Jarrow, dedicated to St Paul. N.J. Higham, *The Kingdom of Northumbria AD 350–1100* (Alan Sutton Publishing Ltd., 1993).
16 Aidan MacDonald, *Curadán, Boniface and the early church of Rosemarkie* (Groam House Museum Trust, 1992), discusses in depth connections between 'Boniface' and the northern territories of the Picts. 'Boniface', the English form of the Roman Bonifacious = 'one who speaks well' was one adopted by numerous Popes of the early centuries. Boniface V, died 625, had had a particular concern for England and Northumbria. On commissioning Wynfrith of Devon as his agent in Germany, Pope Gregory II gave him the name Boniface under which he was to be martyred in Frisia in 754. Aidan MacDonald suggests that the adoption of a Roman name by Curitán, bishop of Ross, was in keeping with his catholicising policy, and that the name 'Boniface' associated with his mission probably also reflects Pope Boniface V as

the patron of the Northumbrian Church. Jocelyn Rendall, *St Boniface Kirk* (Papay Publications n.d.) suggests, however, that the Papay Kirk was dedicated in memory of the Apostle of Germany. I suspect that that was probably not so – the martyrdom is somewhat late – and think MacDonald's version more likely, the identity of name reflecting the similarity of policy.

17 trans. Leo Sherley-Price, *Bede: a History of the English Church and People* (Penguin Classics, 1955) pp. 309-22.

18 Raymond Lamb, 'Papil, Picts and Papar' in ed. Barbara E. Crawford, *Northern Isles Connections* (The Orkney Press, Kirkwall, 1995).

19 Gordon Donaldson, *Faith of the Scots* (London, 1990) pp.16-24. Gordon Donaldson, a senior Scottish Episcopalian layman and before he died HM Historiographer in Scotland, in fact denied that 'Christianity ever permeated the nation'. He believed in 'an active force of evil', as a result of which 'criminal violence as well as disorders like drunkenness . . . have been endemic over the centuries'. Nevertheless, 'each generation has had its committed Christians.' (p.146).

20 Anna Ritchie, *Exploring Scotland's Heritage – Orkney* (The Stationery Office, 1996) nos. 44, 46.

21 Christopher Morris, 'The chapel and enclosure on the Brough of Deerness, Orkney: survey and excavations, 1975-77', in *Proc. Soc. Antiq. Scot.* (1986). See below.

22 Anthony Jackson, *The Symbol Stones of Scotland* (The Orkney Press, 1984) pp.7-8 contains interesting speculation on the early relations between Orkney and Picts further south.

23 John Hunter, *A Persona for the Northern Picts* (Groam House Museum, 1997) discusses excavations at Howe (Stromness), Skaill (Deerness) and Pool (Sanday).

24 Peter Brown, *The Rise of Western Christendom* (Oxford, 1996) p.227.

25 Anna Ritchie, 'Birsay around AD 800' in *Orkney Heritage* vol.2 (Kirkwall, 1983) p.56.

26 Alfred P. Smyth, op. cit. (1984) p.85.

27 Donald Smith, *Celtic Travellers – Scotland in the age of the Saints*, (HMSO, 1997).

28 Visitors have been struck by the Chapel since Jo Ben in the sixteenth century. It has been the focus of pilgrimage and superstition; it has been archaeologically excavated and surveyed on several occasions. The most recent report is that by Prof. Christopher Morris and a team from the University of Durham, op. cit. Among its findings, this Report notes . . .
- The finding of an Anglo-Saxon silver penny minted AD 959-75, such as was commonly present in Norse hoards.
- Besides the Chapel (with its surrounding enclosure) the site includes a well, numerous rectangular buildings, and a screening wall to landward.
- The possibility of circular dwellings is not discounted, though wartime damage by shell-fire makes it difficult to be precise!
- The Chapel as we see it, built in stone, is dated to the Norse period. However, there is evidence that it was preceded by a timber-built Chapel.
- Radio-carbon dating from the Chapel's enclosure suggests occupation as early as

AD 730 (with a 90 year margin of error either way).
Professor Morris:
> *Without the radiocarbon date, there is little to prevent an argument being put forward that the site's history could be wholly encompassed within the Norse period. With the radiocarbon date, it would be likelier that the Timber Phase was pre-Norse... Disuse of the chapel could then, perhaps, be seen as during the period while the Norse were pagan, with refoundation of the chapel once conversion to Christianity took place. The Stone Chapel is most unlikely to have been built before the 11th century and could have been built later.*

The Chapel ruins probably therefore do represent a place used for Christian worship since the Celtic period built first in timber and then in stone. But questions remain:
- The Chapel is sited 'off shore', if not on an island at least on a peninsula; does this reflect the locations of both Iona and Lindisfarne 'at arm's length' from the royal centres of power of their day?
- Why, despite the remains of several buildings surrounding the Chapel, is there evidence of no more than six graves?
- Why does tradition from the Middle Ages and beyond not hand down a dedication for the Chapel? Why have no cross-fragments been found?
- What sort of community did the Chapel serve?
  > Was it ever a 'monastery' in the full sense of a permanent, self-sufficient residence for monks and others under an abbot?
  > Was it originally a 'desert in the ocean' – a temporary place of prayer for the voyagers like Cormac, occupied during the summer while the seas were open?
  > Did some later Norse farmer take over the 'place of prayer' and build his farmstead with its private Chapel on the Brough?
  > Is the idea of a 'monastery' simply a 19th century romantic invention?

Professor Morris sums up:
> Iron-age promontory fort, early Christian monastic site, Viking/Norse secular site with associated Chapel, and Norse monastic settlement all remain possibilities, and indeed are not mutually exclusive.

29 D.P. Thomson, *Orkney through the Centuries – Lights and Shadows of the Church's life in the Northern Isles* (Perth, 1956) p.1.

30 I owe the following account to Isobel Clouston.
    Ships serving the Northern Isles have traditionally been named after Northern Saints. As Ninian used to be thought the first evangelist of Orkney, a ship was named after him. The *St Ninian* used to sail to and from Aberdeen, Orkney and Shetland. In February 1903, in poor visibility, she grounded on a sand bank quite near Deerness Parish Kirk. She was successfully refloated and continued on to Kirkwall. The then minister of Deerness, Rev. John McM. Ramsay, suggested that the crew and passengers of the *St Ninian* should donate a bell for the belfry of the Kirk as an expression of their thanks for a safe arrival – suggesting that in time of

fog in future, the bell might be rung as a warning. The bell was duly donated. When the Parish and the United Free congregations were united in Deerness in 1931, Rev. Harald Mooney suggested that the Parish Kirk, formerly known as St Mary's, should be renamed St Ninian's on account of its bell. Mr Mooney was a keen historian of Orkney, and no doubt was also pleased to celebrate the missionary saint, Ninian, after whom the ship was named.

31 Alan Macquarrie, op. cit.
32 Selected verses from Hymn 398 in *The Church Hymnary, Third Edition* (Oxford University Press, 1973).
34 *Songs of God's People* (Oxford University Press, 1988).
34 Mary Low, *Celtic Christianity and Nature* (Edinburgh University Press, 1996) p.3.
35 Alexander Carmichael, *Carmina Gadelica* (Edinburgh, 1899 and subsequent editions) no. 334, p.303.
36 *Common Order* (St Andrews Press, Edinburgh, 1994).
37 Ian Bradley, op. cit. (1993) p.121.

Chapter 3

The 'Conversion' of the Norse – AD 995

The world of the Pictish Kingdom of Orkney was shattered by the Viking raids of the late eighth century.[1] An Irish writer whose focus was Hebridean recorded that 'all the islands of Britain' were attacked in 794. Dicuil, a monk from Iona who fled to Ireland when Columba's monastery was attacked, later wrote that he remembered from his youth the tales of monk-voyagers who had withdrawn from the northern islands because of 'the northman-pirates'.[2] Vikings came for pillage – gold and slaves. Though pagans who despised the peaceful Christian clergy, raiders no doubt initially left alone those who were of no value and did not get in their way. Perhaps this initial period of raiding is the context for the story of the escape from Vikings to an Orkney monastic community (perhaps on Papa Westray?) of the Irish saint Findan.[3] Nevertheless, the church must have echoed a new prayer: *A furore nordmannorum, libera nos, domine*; From the fury of the north men, O Lord, deliver us.[4]

It seems that from early in the ninth century, Orkney had become an integral part of the Norse world. Various ship-borne warriors utilised the islands as a base for further raiding and colonisation of the Western Isles and Ireland, and down both the east and west coasts of Scotland and England. From Orkney, too, longships could sail on to Iceland, Greenland and Vinland. Orkney was central to the Norse Empire of the Western Ocean; it became an Earldom, to be held only by the powerful. The *Orkneyinga Saga*[5] recounts the legendary deeds of the first earls of Orkney of the Norwegian family of More. Earl Sigurd the Mighty (died *c*.893) together with Thorstein the Red had conquered a vast area in

Sutherland, Caithness, Moray and Ross by the later ninth century.

Quite how sudden and how violent was the Norse arrival in Orkney? Such facts as are available are largely provided by archaeologists, whose reports of excavations are professionally cautious and often uncompleted. Sites may only be partially explored, or in some way may be atypical. It is now common, however, to speak of an 'interface' period, when items and indications of both Pictish and Norse derivation may be found. Some farm mounds, like that at Pool, Sanday, appear to have been in continuous occupation from prehistoric times. It might be expected that farmers using basically the same technology, though of different culture, might appreciate equally locations with good land and a supply of building materials.[6] Norse society in the heroic period utilised slave labour. Although slaves could be treated harshly, they had economic value – after an initial onslaught it would make no sense for incoming warriors to kill off people (especially if female) with local knowledge and skills to be used, if kept in place and in their place.[7] Incoming conquerors throughout history target for immediate occupation places of significance and power; from the arrival of the Norse on the agriculturally unproductive Brough of Birsay this, too, appears to have been a feature of the occupation of Orkney.[8] If (as some evidence suggests) the local Orcadian rulers had been at variance with the mainland Pictish royal power, it is even possible they had initially welcomed Vikings as mercenary warriors, much as the British king Vortigern had attempted to use Saxon allies. Raiding – trading – short-lived alliances – deliberate conquest: probably they all played a part, until Norse authority became overwhelming. Once the newcomers were established, however, they rebuilt their farms to their own, clearly identifiable, patterns.[9] Dr Raymond Lamb suggests the following summary of events:[10]

- The new Norse rulers of Orkney took over as a ruling class, subjugating the existing inhabitants;
- Confiscating the lands of the 'Papar', the Pictish clergy;
- Staging a revival of the old Norse religion to celebrate their success and justify their seizures.

The Orkney Islands were part of the Kingdom of Norway for some three hundred years. Whatever language was spoken by the original inhabitants, it was displaced by Norn. Place-name studies show the extent of the transformation, and also provide some evidence for the practice of the old religion. Gregor Lamb suggests that the mid-summer fire festival was practised in Orkney; and finds reference in old names to the gods Thor, Inga/Freyr and Odin/Grimr, as well as to trolls and giants.[11] There is, however, the suggestion that in the folk-tales of the Northern Isles something of the pre-Norse peoples survived, passed on from mother to child.[12]

The Pictish Church of the eighth century was closely identified with royal power – so much so that a series of kings of the mainland Pictish realm were named for the first Christian Roman Emperor Constantine. A later generation could think of the church being 'in servitude' in Pictish times. It could hardly be expected, therefore, that the institutional structures of the church in Orkney would survive the destruction of Pictish power. There would have been an imperative political necessity, quite besides the likelihood of ecclesiastical treasure to seize and lands to appropriate. One twelfth century account was that the Picts and the 'Papar' (the ruling class and their priests?) were eradicated.[13] A sense of the holy, however, is harder to burn than wood and wattle; it cannot be easily stolen, like gold and silver. The success of Dr Lamb's thesis, moreover, depends on the survival from the eighth century, at least in the memory of *people*, of the dedications of churches to St Peter – or, on Papay, to Sts Boniface and Triduana. He suggests, therefore, that though weakened, some aspects of the church managed to survive.[14] Similarly, the name Eynhallow is thought to suggest a continuing reverence for an existing sacred place. Westness, Rousay, is a good example of a Pictish cemetery that continued in use, with the incoming Norse respecting Pictish Christian graves.[15]

Paganism was out-of-date, however, even in northern Europe, in the century after the death of Charlemagne. The Christian Kings of Europe set the standards for monarchy. Besides, the Viking era had brought to Scandinavia, besides Christian wealth, Christian slaves and Christian ideas. In 995 King Olaf Tryggvasson of Norway converted to 'the faith of the White Christ' whilst raiding England, and attempted to enforce his decision wherever his fleet sailed.

> Olaf Tryggvasson sailed east with five ships and didn't break his journey until he reached Orkney. At Osmundwall he ran into Earl Sigurd who

had three ships and was setting out on a viking expedition. Olaf sent a messenger to him asking Sigurd to come over to his ship as he wanted a word with him. 'I want you and all your subjects to be baptised. If you refuse, I'll have you killed on the spot and I swear that I'll ravage every island with fire and steel.' The Earl could see what kind of a situation he was in and surrendered himself into Olaf's hands. After that, all Orkney embraced the faith. (*The Orkneyinga Saga*).

What, however, are we to make of such a 'conversion'?[16] Certainly King Olaf had submitted to baptism and displayed the convert's enthusiasm for his new faith; but it is difficult to understand how a Christianity with any authentic allegiance to the Jesus of the New Testament can be transmitted by threats of death. Besides, the supposedly converted Earl was to die later in battle under the Raven banner of his pagan predecessors. Nevertheless, despite the personalities of the rulers, the 'conversion' meant that the Faith's institutions in Roman forms returned to Orkney after 995. Christian clerics possibly already had a place in the Earl's household – his wife, mother and grandmother had come from Christian cultures. Bishops began to appear who related to the rest of the Christian world, having obtained consecration from archbishops who themselves looked to Rome.[17]

Throughout Norse Orkney, farms and settlements came to include a chapel: their own place of worship. Sites of hundreds of chapels have been identified, and can be traced through archaeological surveys. Farmstead and church or chapel went together, it seems, throughout the early Norse Christian world. Important Orcadian examples are:

- St Nicholas' round Church, Orphir and the Earl's drinking hall
- Kolbein Hruga's castle, Wyre and St Mary's Chapel
- Cross Kirk, Westray and the Tuquoy site
- The church and hall at Skaill, Deerness.

These local chapels – there were at least 140 of them – predated the creation of a formal parish system. As dating their remains is a high risk business, they may, in fact, have also predated the official 'conversion' of Earl Sigurd. Places of worship – perhaps buildings, perhaps simply hallowed by tradition – do seem in some (a few?) cases to have survived the pagan times from Orkney's first Christian period. Essentially, however, each Christian farm or settlement built its own chapel, and, presumably, sustained its own priest or curate. It is not thought that, in the main, these were on sites hallowed by the Pictish church. Neither is the older suggestion so readily accepted that each chapel served a taxation unit, the urisland, and that these derived from Pictish administrative groupings.[18] The creation of the network of chapels was due, primarily, to the desire of the new Norse population of Orkney to sponsor Christian worship.

Earl Thorfinn II, the Mighty (died 1065), attempted to create a realm for himself stretching from Shetland to the Isle of Man, and including most of northern Scotland. Not only a warrior, he also gave attention to the administrative and legal aspects of government. He is credited by the Sagas with the institution of the Norse Bishopric. It is thought that Thorfinn himself visited Rome and obtained Papal authority for the institution of one Thorolf as Bishop of Orkney, within the archdiocese of Hamburg.

> By now he was finished with piracy and devoted all his time to the government of his people and country and to the making of new laws. He had his permanent residence at Birsay where he built and dedicated to Christ a fine minster, which was the first seat of the Orkney Bishopric. (*The Orkneyinga Saga*).

Again, however, the Saga-poet's account should not be swallowed whole. Archaeologists are quite willing to identify as Christian Norse the cemetery at Saevar Howe, Birsay, and to date this community before Earl Thorfinn's time.[19] Professor Per Sveaas Andersen notes that, while Thorolf was the first Bishop in Orkney with a permanent seat, complete with estates, revenues and cathedral, he had had predecessors. The earliest bishops had functioned something like personal chaplains to the kings and earls, travelling with their courts and dependent on their sponsors. Only when a permanent seat was established and endowed could the distinctive Catholic institutions come into existence: a bishop with a chapter of senior clergy supporting and maintaining a daily routine of worship together with the administration of discipline within a diocese.[20] Moreover, another early source, the churchman Adam of

Bremen, of the household of the archbishop of Hamburg, in also telling of the appointment of a bishop at Birsay, mentions that previous bishops in Orkney had been English or Scottish. Before Rome gave Hamburg jurisdiction over the north and before the creation of the archdioceses of either St Andrews or Nideros, the Archbishop of York claimed Orkney as within his see. Adam further recounts that one Henry, treasurer to King Cnut of England (before 1035) had been Bishop in Orkney.[21] Without a diocesan seat, however, such appointments were unlikely to have been more than nominal – if, indeed, these bishops ever came north at all. It was easy for the Saga poets to rewrite history as they sought to emphasise the achievements of their heroes – the Christian kings, earls and saints of the Norse heroic age. It may also be that the Sagas reflect the Catholicism of the Rome of Pope Innocent III (1160-1216), with its heightened sense of its institutional authority, in thinking in terms of 'conversion', *'embracing the faith'*, to describe this process of a people, perhaps already many nominally (or even substantially) Christian, being admitted to the structures of a Church centred on Rome.

Once the formal structure of the Catholic Church had returned to Orkney, besides the local chapels one might expect to find the monastic communities that had elsewhere for centuries been an important way of fulfilling spiritual needs. Unfortunately it is difficult for archaeologists to distinguish on the basis of structural remains between a *farming* community with its own chapel, and a *monastic* community – for such would also have a chapel and live by farming. In her 1996 survey of Orkney's historic monuments, Anna Ritchie accepts the likelihood that the chapel on Eynhallow was monastic in the early Norse period and mentions the possibility that that on Birsay was monastic. The Chapel on the Brough of Deerness she suggests was a domestic place of worship and not monastic; at Papa Westray, she simply notes that St Boniface Kirk continued in use in Norse times. Others more strongly advocate the monastic claims of their candidate.[22]

One further institution of the Church that some identify in early Norse Christian Orkney is the minster, a church that functioned with a team of priests and that served as an episcopal base among others before a single Cathedral became accepted. Thorfinn's death left Orkney under the rule of joint-earls Paul and Erlend, and they were succeeded by their sons, Hakon and Magnus. The two cousins, however, proved unable to co-operate; each sponsored their own client Bishop of Orkney, looking as was convenient to either York or Hamburg for consecration of their client. It is suggested that Earl Magnus, whose lands included Birsay and its Christchurch Cathedral, sought recognition from York and Rome of Bishop Ralph Novell. The bishop in power in Orkney, however, was William the Old, whose home church appears from the Sagas to have been on Egilsay. It may, therefore, have been to a minster on Egilsay, that the two Earls Hakon and Magnus came to settle their differences in Easter week, 1115.[23]

Hakon, however, came with eight ships instead of the agreed two. Rather than plunge the islands into warfare, Magnus gave himself up.

> Once it had been decided that the saintly Earl Magnus was to die, Hakon told his standard bearer Ofeig to do the killing, but he refused angrily; so Hakon ordered his cook Lifilf to kill Magnus. 'Stand in front of me and strike me hard on the head,' said Magnus, 'it's not fitting for a chieftain to be beheaded like a thief. Take heart – I've prayed that God grant you his mercy.' (*The Orkneyinga Saga*).

Hakon's line did not rule Orkney unchallenged, however. Magnus' nephew Rognvald came to power *c*.1136 assisted by the spreading stories of miracles worked through the influence of his saintly uncle.

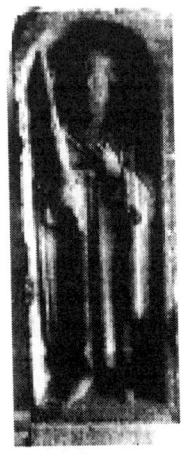

15th century statue of St Magnus from Kirkwall Cathedral

Rognvald began the building of a great new church in his patron's honour, the Cathedral of St Magnus, at Kirkwall. During the lengthy episcopate of William the Old (died 1168), the seat of the diocese was transferred from Birsay to Kirkwall.

Though on a smaller scale, St Magnus Cathedral appears to have been influenced by masons from the great Norman Cathedral of Durham. It is still the most magnificent building in Kirkwall. Other church buildings of significance survive from the years of Norse dominance. Earl Hakon Paulsson, Magnus' slayer, went on a pilgrimage to the Holy Land. He was probably responsible for the round church at Orphir, St Nicholas', whose design echoed the Church of the Holy Sepulchre at Jerusalem.[24] The remains of the Church on the Brough of Birsay date from the twelfth century and are described by Barbara Crawford as 'the oldest and most impressive church ruin of its date in northern or western Scotland'.[25] On Egilsay itself, a church named for Magnus was built or rededicated in the mid-twelfth century. It is now the sole example of a round-towered church in Orkney. Other church buildings that may date from the twelfth century are: St Mary's Chapel, Wyre; Cross Kirk, Westray; the unnamed chapel on the Brough of Deerness; St Boniface Church, Papa Westray. At Deerness (in St Ninian's Church) and at St Boniface Kirk on Papay are also examples of 'hogback' gravestones, shaped like a roof-ridge and carved complete with roof-tiles.[26] The hogback design originated in the hinterland of the great Norse trading city of York. York – Durham – Hamburg – Rome – Jerusalem: the 'conversion' of the Norse facilitated Orkney's lines of communication throughout Christian Europe.

Even though the church had been part of Orkney's culture before 995, the impact of the 'conversion' of Norse Orkney to the Christian Faith should not be assumed to be minimal.[27] The Faith brought with it a new set of values and ideals – often quite contrary to those supported by the pagan gods. Though Christian states continued to put criminals to death for centuries, the horrific ritual torture of the blood-eagle ended with the cult of Odin. If any state had chosen to remain pagan it would presumably have had quite different concepts of justice and law from those accepted in Christendom. The death of Earl Magnus, presented as a form of martyrdom to prevent civil war, assisted the propagation of values quite different from those of the Viking warriors of earlier years. Over the centuries, the Church with some success sought to limit the effects of warfare to those bearing arms, and the rise of Christianity in the Norse lands also saw an end to the trade in captives as slaves. Some of the energy formerly spent in raiding the shores of Ireland and Britain was now directed to pilgrimage (and to crusade) to Jerusalem. In politics, however, ideals regularly come off second-best when real power is at stake; disputes, betrayals and killings continued for decades and centuries seemingly unchecked after 995, to fill the pages of the *Orkneyinga Saga*.

What of those whose taxes paid for the building of St Magnus and of the other churches and chapels – what of the ordinary people of Orkney? *Magnus' Saga*[28] tells that, increasingly, when farmers and their families found themselves in trouble, they brought their troubles to Magnus at his shrine and found their difficulties overcome. Petitioning the Saint for defence and remedy was akin to petitioning the Earl for justice – and often no less effective! The Saga lists cures from insanity, leprosy, a fractured skull, blindness, crippled hands . . . The Christianised Norse also turned to others for assistance: throughout the northern and western isles the name of Columba retained its power. So, too, did the shrine on Papa Westray associated with Triduana, to whose Well came those seeking healing for their sight. The cult of Magnus, however, is the first distinctively Orcadian contribution to the long Christian tradition.[29]

> O Magnus of my love,
> Thou it is who would'st us guide.
> Thou fragrant body of grace,
> Remember us.
>
> Remember us, thou Saint of power,
> Who didst encompass and protect the people,
> Succour us in our distress,
> Nor forsake us.
>
> Lift our flocks to the hills,
> Quell the wolf and the fox,
> Ward from us spectre, giant, fury,
> And oppression.

> O Magnus of fame,
> On the barque of the heroes,
> On the crest of the waves,
> On the sea, on the land,
> Aid and preserve us.

The Christian faith thus provided some security and hope to all, not just to kings and warriors. The Faith kept at bay the powers of chaos: monsters, trolls. . . . It underpinned a sense of justice; bound together Orkney with the European world – with Christendom.

> The world of order; the world of human settlement defined in sharp contrast to the wild; the world identified in aristocratic epic with the bright halls of the chieftains and, on a humbler level, with the tilled fields . . .: all this could be seen as now lying under the protection of Christ. Christian rituals upheld that world. Christian kings ruled it.[30]

Thus, in exchange, under the protection of the Norse Earls of Orkney, the Church's organisation and structures flourished.[31] The period opens the way to one of the key features of contemporary Orcadian society – the Parish. More than any other area of Scotland, Orcadians are still conscious of the parish in which they live – not necessarily as a religious but as a social unit. A 'Parish Cup' is competed for between football teams; BBC Radio Orkney broadcasts programmes called 'The Heart of the Parish'. The SWRI and other organisations remain parish-based. But the concept of the 'parish' was at first a Christian one.

The spiritual responsibility for all the people of a diocese was and is given by the Roman Catholic Church to its bishop. However, western Europe came to adopt the 'parish system' by which bishops placed priests in subdivisions of the diocese, each area a parish with its own church. The Christian kingdoms of the west enforced at law the duty of all residents to pay the tithe – a tenth of all produce – to support their parish church. In mainland Scotland, King David I (1124-53) regularised these payments and the parish system was completed about 1200. In Norway, King Sigurd (died 1130) was the first actively to enforce the raising of tithe. Belonging to the Faith, in the Christian West, was an act of royal policy – as it had been in the days of the Roman Empire after Constantine. All were compelled to support the church by the payment of the tithe.[32]

How old are Orkney's parishes? Before these church groupings existed, households in Orkney were organised by the earls into administrative units that served as a basis for raising 'scat' – taxing the people. These family units were named 'ploughlands' when a tax of one mark each was levied by Earl Rognvald for the construction of St Magnus. Other words for such groupings were used. Later the term 'pennyland' came into being with the imposition after 1153 in Norway and its colonies of a levy for the Papacy known as 'Peter's Pence'. The terms 'tunship' and 'ouncelands' or 'urislands' were also used in the context of scat. It has been suggested that the earls may well have based these local groupings on the patterns of farms and settlements that the Norse inherited from the Pictish Kingdom; and that the later church groupings for convenience followed the same patterns.[33] If this was so, then the boundaries of Orkney's parishes would indeed be ancient, going back to the farms and settlements of pre-history. It should be said, however, that this thesis is discounted by Professor Per Sveaas Andersen who argues that, throughout the Norse lands, churches were built originally not according to any set pattern but simply as private chapels by those who wanted and could afford them.[34] The later parish system would then have been influenced by the speed and depth of the 'conversion' of the various Norse landholders, with the major Christian families seeking parish status for their chapels. Yet Orkney, unlike the other Norse lands, had had a Christian past before the Norse arrived. . . .

The parishes, then, as we know them historically, came into being during the twelfth century: local areas, grouped together to pay tithe, supporting their own Church and priest – living and worshipping together. Whether or not the areas as we know them had predecessors before the Catholic Church created its parishes, a powerful sense of belonging to a parish and its community was created in the people of Orkney; a sense that has endured through the generations. That it is now under challenge is a significant cause of unease. The local mills are in ruins – redundant. Rural parish schools have already closed or amalgamated. The population's drift to Kirkwall seems unstoppable. Country shops cannot compete with Kirkwall's larger supermarkets and petrol stations – and the ro-ro ferry service means that even island shops are threatened. The car has removed the focus of life from the parish – but try to close a Parish Church, and see what a turmoil arises. After all, among other issues, at least eight hundred years of tradition are at stake.

1 I was appointed Interim Moderator of the southern isles charge of Hoy and Walls with Flotta in 1994, when Rev. Graham Monteith retired. One of the last acts of the Kirk Session of Hoy and Walls with Graham as Moderator was to recommend that the coming year, 1995, include a celebration of the millennium of the conversion of the Norse to Christianity. The key meeting in AD 995 between the then King of Norway and Earl of Orkney had taken place at sea off Osmundwall, round the shore of South Walls from Longhope – an old chapel and burial ground still mark the site. I found myself committed, together with the Session, to implementing the decision – especially as the Presbytery's Mission Resources Committee, when approached, was pleased to allow Hoy and Walls to take the lead in these preparations. An opportunity to think about Orkney's Norse years was welcome. At my formal Introduction to the Presbytery during a service at St Magnus Cathedral, the then Moderator, Rev. Bill Cant, had spoken of Magnus, his example and influence; my interest had been stirred.

Hoy and Walls were, however, not the only group in Orkney that had spotted the importance of 995. Orkney is twinned with the region of Hordaland in Norway, and an active Liaison Committee was sponsored by Orkney Islands Council. The danger was that the well-resourced and influential Council body would by-pass or marginalise the plans of Hoy and Walls' Session. After some initial misunderstandings, both Ron Ferguson, minister at St Magnus Cathedral, Kirkwall, and I were co-opted to the Liaison Committee. My Department of National Mission provided the Session with a small financial subsidy to help with expenses; the Orkney Tourist Board also promised financial support for an event that was likely to help extend the tourist season. A good deal of hard work was also done by the congregation of Hoy and Walls, and by North Walls School.

When it came, the 'Norse weekend', 9-11 June, attracted considerable interest and support. Three Norwegian naval patrol vessels paid a visit to Kirkwall and provided a Guard of Honour at the main act of worship at St Magnus Cathedral on the Sunday, at which the Bishop of Nideros, Rt. Rev. Finn Wagle, preached; and also for an evening service at the Norwegian war graves in the burial ground. The Presbytery sponsored a public lecture on the 'Conversion' with key historians participating: Dr Barbara E. Crawford of St Andrews University, a specialist on Orkney's mediaeval history; Dr Raymond Lamb, then Orkney Heritage Society's archaeologist, and Per Sveaas Andersen, a retired Norwegian professor, specialist on Norway's western colonies. Planned for the Supper Room of Kirkwall Community Centre, the crowds attending quickly moved to fill the old Kirkwall Council Chamber. A new book was published, ed. Barbara E. Crawford, *Northern Isles Connections: Essays from Orkney and Shetland presented to Per Sveaas Andersen* (The Orkney Press, 1995 – limited edition); and the 'presentation' itself took place at the public meeting to considerable acclaim.

Also visiting Orkney for the Norse weekend were the Norwegian Ambassador to the UK and the regular meeting of Norway's British consuls. These provided the occasion for a 're-enactment' of the meeting of King Hakon of Norway and Earl Sigurd of Orkney. The consuls, while touring Scapa Flow courtesy of Elf Enterprise, met at sea off Osmundwall with the Houton-Lyness ferry carrying the Convener of Orkney Islands Council and a good number of folk from Hoy and Walls. The two key 'players', the Bishop of Nideros and the Convener, were exchanged between the 'Norwegians' and the 'Orcadians'. The consuls continued their tour; the Bishop, and Professor Andersen, went in to Longhope, where the Bishop brought greetings from his Cathedral of Trondheim to the island's congregation at St Columba's Church. Tea followed in the YM Hall, where there was an exhibition for the day with items from the island and also from some of Orkney's Primary Schools. Later in the year, Hoy and Walls also had their own commemorative Sunday service, with the Very Rev. Dr James Weatherhead, former Principal Clerk to the General Assembly, as guest preacher.

The events did not pass without criticism. Besides a South Walls demonstrator against Norwegian whaling, the *Orcadian* published a letter pointing out that the 'conversion' had been achieved by threats of laying the islands waste, and by taking as hostage one of Earl Sigurd's sons. The latter, Hundi, moreover, appears to have died or disappeared while a captive in Norway. What sort of Christianity was this, the letter asked, that took children hostage? Why celebrate such an event? Further, there was the important point that Orkney had not been straightforwardly pagan before 995. Dr Raymond Lamb's contributions to both the public lecture and the book emphasised all the evidence for a Pictish church before ever the Norse arrived. Conscious that the original events were – at best – ambiguous, I therefore preferred to use the word 'commemorate' rather than 'celebrate'. The idea of the public lecture was also to explore the meaning of the supposed 'conversion' of 995. The Cathedral order of service, however, was headed 'Celebration of the Millennium of Christianity in Norway'. This chapter takes up these issues: it contains much that Orcadians will already know. My debt to Dr Raymond Lamb, Dr Barbara Crawford, Prof. Per Sveaas Andersen, William P.L. Thomson and other Orcadian historians will be obvious to those who have read their books. Barbara E. Crawford, *Scandinavian Scotland* (Leicester University Press, 1987) is a standard work. William P.L. Thomson, *History of Orkney* (Edinburgh, 1987) is the authoritative single volume history.

2   Alfred P. Smyth, op. cit. pp.167-73.
3   Jocelyn Rendall, *St Boniface Kirk* (Papay Publications, n.d.) citing William P.L.

Thomson, op.cit. pp. 39-40.
4 John Marsden, *The Fury of the Northmen – Saints, Shrines and Sea-raiders in the Viking Age* (London, 1996).
5 ed. Joseph Anderson, *The Orkneyinga Saga* (1873 reprinted Edinburgh 1990 and other editions).
6 John Hunter, op.cit.; Hunter, Bond, Smith, 'Some aspects of early Viking settlement in Orkney' in ed. Batey, Jesch, Morris, *The Viking Age in Caithness, Orkney and the North Atlantic* (Edinburgh University Press, 1995).
7 Anna Ritchie, 'Birsay around AD 800' (1983) pp. 63-4. Written evidence for thralls in Orkney itself is, unfortunately, tenuous: Barbara E. Crawford, op.cit. (1987) pp.210-11.
8 Anna Ritchie, *Viking Scotland* (Historic Scotland/B.T. Batsford, 1993) pp. 52-4.
9 Barbara E. Crawford, op.cit. (1987) pp.139-48.
10 Raymond G. Lamb, 'Papil, Picts and Papar', op.cit. (1995).
11 Gregor Lamb, *Testimony of the Orkneyinga – The Placenames of Orkney* (Orkney, 1993).
12 Anna Ritchie, 'Birsay around AD 800' (1983) p. 64.
13 Barbara E. Crawford, op.cit. (1987) pp.56, 210-11.
14 Raymond G. Lamb, 'Carolingian Orkney and its Transformation' in ed. Batey, Jesch, Morris, op.cit. pp. 260-9.
15 Sigrid H.H. Kaland, 'The settlement of Westness, Rousay' in ed. Batey, Jesch, Morris, op.cit. pp. 312-17.
16 The saga-story is described as 'in the highest degree implausible' by Richard Fletcher, *The Barbarian Conversion: from paganism to Christianity* (Henry Holt and Company, 1997) p. 378. But the story has its own power and continues to be told . . .
17 Barbara E. Crawford, op.cit. (1987) pp. 68-71.
18 Barbara E. Crawford, op.cit. (1987) pp.180-4. Per Sveaas Andersen, 'The Orkney Church of the Twelfth and Thirteenth Centuries – a Stepdaughter of the Norwegian Church?' in ed. B.E. Crawford, *St Magnus Cathedral and Orkney's 12th-Century Renaissance* (1988).
19 Christopher D. Morris, 'The Birsay Bay project – a resumé', in ed. Batey, Jesch, Morris, op.cit. pp. 286-7.
20 Per Sveaas Andersen, op.cit. (1988).
21 William P.L. Thomson, op.cit. pp. 52-3; Barbara E. Crawford, 'Birsay and the early Earls and Bishops of Orkney' in *Orkney Heritage* vol. 2 (Kirkwall, 1983) pp.102-6.
22 Anna Ritchie, op.cit. (1996) nos. 44, 46, 48, 49. See also the highly speculative: John Mooney, *Eynhallow, the Holy Island of the Orkneys* (Kirkwall, 1923). C.A. Ralegh Radford, 'Birsay and the Spread of Christianity in the North' in *Orkney Heritage* vol. 2 (Kirkwall, 1983) envisages a small Celtic monastic settlement on the Brough of Birsay before the Norse, and a small Norse monastic community on Eynhallow after the 'conversion'.

22 Barbara E. Crawford, 'Birsay and the early Earls and Bishops of Orkney' (1983) pp. 106-110; C.A. Ralegh Radford, op.cit.
24 Ian Fisher, 'Orphir Church in its South Scandinavian Context' in ed. Batey, Jesch, Morris, op.cit.
25 Barbara E. Crawford, op.cit. (1987) pp.178-90.
26 Anna Ritchie, *Exploring Scotland's Heritage – Orkney* (1996) nos. 39, 49, 41, 42, 43, 46, 47, 48.
27 Barbara E. Crawford, op.cit. (1987) pp.68-71.
28 trans. Palsson/Edwards, *Magnus' Saga – The life of St Magnus, Earl of Orkney 1075–1116* (Perpetua Press, 1987).
29 From *Carmina Gadelica*, op.cit. no. 72 p. 82.
30 Peter Brown, op.cit. (1996) p. 315.
31 Ian B. Cowan, 'The medieval bishops of St Magnus' in ed. Cant/Firth, *Light in the North* (Orkney Press, 1989).
32 Ian B. Cowan, 'The Development of the Parochial System' in ed. James Kirk, *The Medieval Church in Scotland* (Scottish Academic Press, 1995).
33 Gregor Lamb, op.cit. p. 63 also speculates that the overall pattern of parishes has a strong trinitarian basis.
34 Per Sveaas Andersen, op.cit. (1988).

Chapter 4

Catholic and Protestant; Episcopalian and Presbyterian: 1540-1715

During the Catholic Era, the influence of Norway waned and that of Scotland grew over Orkney. From the days of William the Lion, King of Scots 1143-1214, the southern kingdom's authority was extended to Caithness, so that Earls of Orkney came to own a dual allegiance: to Norway, for their Orkney lands; and to Scotland for Caithness.[1] Involvement by the men of Orkney with Scottish affairs continued through the latter's Wars of Independence from England. From the thirteenth century, from the time of Earl Magnus II, the ruling house in Orkney was of Scots rather than Norse birth. In church terms, matters were further confused by the existence of two rival Popes – one line of which was recognised by, among others, Norway; and the other by Scotland. Increasingly, bishops of Orkney were drawn from the Scottish priesthood. Plague had meantime decimated the population of Norway, reducing drastically its available clergy – and that kingdom became subject to Denmark. In 1468, Denmark placed the Orkney Islands in pawn to the Crown of Scotland and James III assumed the rights of a feudal Lord of Orkney. In 1472, Rome replaced the jurisdiction of Nidaros over Orkney with that of the Archdiocese of St Andrews – though it took time for Trondheim to come to terms with the Bull.[2]

In his chapter 'The daily life of the Orkneyinga', Gregor Lamb emphasises that such was the importance placed by the parish communities on their church that roads and paths were given names such as 'Kirkgate' ('gate' represents *gata* in Norse and hence 'path') or 'Messigate' from the main service, the Mass. Older beliefs mixed in the popular mind with Catholic spirituality. Stories of trolls and fairies and the Celtic scenery of sacred wells and mounds were also part of ordinary life.³ Pilgrimage to the shrine of St Magnus and to the ancient sacred places, including the old chapels at Birsay and Deerness, also came to be part of the Orcadian practice of the Christian Faith. It may well be that the influence of older lore survived longer in Orkney than in Scotland because of the survival of the Norn language (though in weakened form) to the eighteenth century, maintaining a degree of isolation from modernising influences.⁴

St Magnus Cathedral to this day dominates the Orkney skyline. In the Catholic era, it also dominated the life of the Church. In 1544, Bishop Robert Reid restructured the relationship between his Cathedral, its administration, funding and organisation, and the parishes of his diocese.

A Chapter of fourteen canons was authorised: seven senior clergy, controlling the key aspects of the Cathedral and diocese, and seven prebendaries with lesser responsibilities, mainly the charge of the major chapels within the Cathedral. In addition to these senior priests, the staff of the Cathedral included the chaplains of the other chapels within it, and a choir, assisted by boys at the Cathedral choir school. The daily routine of services was led by the chaplains, junior priests, acting on behalf of the canons; for most of the senior clergy were only required to be resident in Kirkwall for half the year.⁵

Such a large establishment required to be maintained; and the money needed came from the parishes. Bishop Reid regularised and adjusted an already existing system, whereby the bulk of the tithe paid by all of Orkney's parishes went not to the local church but to the Cathedral, for the expenses of the bishopric and to provide stipends for the Chapter. Such an arrangement was quite normal; most of Scotland's parish income was similarly appropriated. The system was one of the basic weaknesses of the Catholic Church in Scotland. The result was an impoverished parish life, with insufficient funds left properly to maintain the structure of the parish churches or to attract and employ the more able of the priesthood.⁶ The bishop himself received the tithes allocated to the rector or parson of the parishes of Papay, Our Lady's in Westray, Eday, St Peter's and Our Lady's in Stronsay, Rousay and Egilsay, Shapinsay, Sandwick, Evie and Rendall, Firth, St Ola, St Andrews and Deerness, Holm, and Flotta. Each parish provided two sources of income: the parson's and the vicar's tithe. The following table shows how these were allocated according to the 1544 restructuring of the diocese. 'Mensal' means 'for the table of the Bishop', or in modern terms, for 'the expenses of the diocese'. 'Expenses' were a valuable 'perk', then as now! Of fifty individual incomes, only eleven remained unappropriated.[7]

	Parsonage	*Vicarage*
North Ronaldsay	Treasurer	FREE
Papa Westray	Mensal	Mensal
Westray: Lady	Mensal	FREE
Westray: Cross	Chancellor	FREE
Sanday: Lady	St Laurence Canon	Chancellor
Sanday: Burness	Subchanter	Chancellor
Sanday: Cross	Holy Cross Canon	Chancellor
Eday	Mensal	united with Stronsay
Stronsay: Lady and Stronsay: St Peter	Mensal	FREE
Stronsay: St Nicholas	Treasurer	FREE (united to Lady/ St Peter)
Rousay and Egilsay	Mensal	FREE
Shapinsay	Mensal	FREE
Birsay and Harray	Archdeacon	Archdeacon
Evie and Rendall	Mensal	Woodwick Canon
Sandwick	Mensal	Held in Common by the Canons
Firth	Mensal	Chanter
Orphir and Stenness	Chanter	Chanter
Stromness	Subchanter	Held in Common by the Canons

St Ola and Kirkwall	Bishop	FREE
St Andrews and Deerness	Mensal	FREE
Holm	Mensal	FREE
Hoy	Subdean	Subdean
Walls	Common for the Canons	Subdean
Flotta	Mensal	Subdean
Burray and St Ronaldsay	Provost	FREE

Who actually provided for the spiritual needs of the parishes of late mediaeval Orkney? If the Cathedral had a staff of fourteen well paid canons who rarely led ordinary worship, Orkney's Parish Churches were the responsibility of another fourteen priests, this time poorly paid and normally in charge of more than one parish. They in turn may have delegated their duties to curates – the least well paid of all clergy. Because so much of the income of the diocese was allocated to the staff of the Cathedral and diocese, it was necessary to unite and link parishes together to find a sufficient income for a priest who actually exercised pastoral responsibility. Thus the islands of Westray, Stronsay and Sanday, supposedly made up of separate parishes, were (with their smaller companions Papay, North Ronaldsay and Eday) considered one charge. Various Mainland parishes were also united. Bishop Reid's 1544 Constitution was to have the consequence of perpetuating this unfortunate system. Each of the following groups of parishes had one priest in charge during the sixteenth century:[8]

> North Ronaldsay, Papa Westray, Westray, Sanday (six parishes)
> Stronsay and Eday (three parishes)
> Rousay (one parish: four islands)
> Shapinsay (one parish)
> Birsay and Harray (two parishes)
> Evie and Rendall (two parishes)
> Firth, Orphir and Stenness (three parishes)
> Sandwick and Stromness (two parishes)
> St Ola inc. Kirkwall (one parish)

St Andrews and Deerness (two parishes)
Holm (one parish)
Burray and South Ronaldsay (three parishes)
Hoy (one parish)
Walls and Flotta (two parishes)

This is, of course, apart from the still-numerous private chapels maintained by the larger landowners. They were often very small – as were the parish churches. The sacrifice of the Mass was thought to shorten the time souls spent in purgatory; the sacrament could only be offered by a priest. Whether or not there was a congregation present to observe had only a limited spiritual meaning – and the service was, of course, conducted in Latin. Churches and chapels, therefore, did not need to be able to seat or house the whole community they served. In the theology of the time, the community they served was largely the community of the dead.

Whether in St Magnus, or the parish churches or the private chapels, the Mass was said or sung many times a week. Priests were supposed to celebrate on a daily basis besides the main public acts of worship. The Christian year contained not just the festivals of Christmas and Easter but also the many days dedicated to the memory of the saints; days sometimes associated with community fairs or processions. The Cathedral contained several altars beside the High Altar – side chapels, with their fitments and chaplains maintained by the crafts or guilds of the town, or by income from lands bequeathed for that purpose. Parish life involved the routine of baptism, confirmation by the bishop, receiving communion at the great Easter celebration, and attending the funerals of neighbours.

In mainland Scotland, when landowners and lords first built a church on their lands, they often retained the right to nominate the priest thus supported by their tithe payments, subject to the rights of bishop and Pope. Very often, they nominated not individuals but monasteries. A complex system grew up, with local revenues often diverted by the patrons to support non-parochial and often distant monasteries and other religious institutions, on condition that they undertook responsibility for the parish's ministry. Thus the monastic system of the Middle Ages also grew out of the tithe, supplemented by voluntary donations and legacies. Orkney, however, is an exception to the Scottish pattern. This county developed its parish system while under Norse rule, and appropriation of tithe was 'relatively rare in Norway during the thirteenth century' according to Professor Per Sveaas Andersen. Control both of appointments and revenues seems to have been obtained from an early time by the bishopric, which may explain why no monastic house seems to have survived in Orkney past the twelfth century.

One possible monastic chapel is the building on the island of Eynhallow which, though domestic by the sixteenth century, may at an earlier date have been monastic. If so, the house had clearly lacked sufficient endowments to continue. Already between 1247 and 1427/8 parish revenues from Sanday, Hoy, Orphir and Stronsay had probably been diverted to the Cathedral. Bishop Reid's reorganisation of the Chapter of St Magnus in 1544 was based on the appropriation of the bulk of parochial revenues from the whole of Orkney to the Cathedral and its staff; nothing was recorded as being due to Eynhallow. In the reorganisation of the parishes after the Reformation, Eynhallow is sometimes listed together with either Rousay, Wyre and Egilsay or with Evie and Rendall as part of a minister's charge. In 1586, Eynhallow appeared, separately from Rousay, Egilsay and Wyre, in a list of churches designated to form the Presbytery of Orkney. Possibly the building enjoyed revived use as an early modern preaching station?[9]

During the long period of unchallenged Catholicism, the Bishops of Orkney enjoyed an equally unchallenged ecclesiastical authority in the county, ruling Chapter and Diocese alike, and administering lands and revenues second only to the Earldom itself. Whereas in Scotland substantial lands, revenues and authority were held by Abbots of such monastic houses as Arbroath, in Orkney the Bishop ruled the church alone. The ruins of the Bishop's Palace in Kirkwall remain as a testimony to the secular power and prestige of its owners. The Church had come a long way from the days of the Celtic voyagers, and their lives of prayer on solitary rock-stack hermitages!

Doctrinally, too, Bishop Reid seems to have had a reasonable grip on Orkney. As well as being a well-educated scholar with a library that still excites envy, Reid was one of the more traditionally Catholic of the higher clergy of his day. He took part in the trial of the Ayshire layman, Adam Wallace, who was burnt for heresy in 1550. One heretic is known to have been in Orkney before the Reformation, James Kaa, a chaplain at the Cathedral, who by 1550 was in exile in England lest he suffer the same fate as Wallace.[10] Reformed opinions, books and literature were being imported into Scotland from the 1540s via the normal processes of trade with the continent and with England. Orkney's harbours and shipping must surely have taken their share of the same theological trade. It is unlikely that Kaa was in fact the only Orcadian whose opinions were diverging from Catholic orthodoxy; the normal procedures of the time were to prosecute formers of opinion, leaders of groups. Indeed, Bishop Reid's new Constitution did attempt to grapple with some of the recognised abuses of the day. In it there is provision for preaching in the vernacular as well as concern for good order, for the maintenance of discipline. Both the Provost and the Archdeacon, the two senior canons, were ordered to 'preach four times a year in the Cathedral Church to the people in the common tongue'. Of all the diocesan and Cathedral posts required by the Constitution, however, these two were the only men required to preach. It was little enough as a response to the demand for the reading, teaching and preaching of the Bible sweeping Europe since Luther's Protest of the 1520s.[11]

The Reformation came to Scotland in 1560. On the death (from illness and age) of the French Regent, Mary of Guise, during an insurrection by Reformed lords and lairds assisted by artillery, infantry and naval forces sent by Elizabeth of England, control of the state fell to the reformers. Parliament met and outlawed the Mass on pain of death. When the youthful Mary, Queen of Scots, arrived from France to exercise personal control of her country and government, events never allowed a restoration of the old religion.

Seal of Adam Bothwell, Bishop of Orkney [from a 19th century photograph]

One of the Regent's last acts had been to secure, in 1559, the appointment by the Pope of Adam Bothwell as Bishop of Orkney. The new Bishop was in his diocese when it became clear that the reforming party, the Lords of the Congregation, had succeeded and that Orkney had joined the world of the Protestant Reformation.[12]

The Scottish Reformed Church, as it developed after the return of Queen Mary, followed a programme that included:[13]

- abolition of the Mass and the authority of the Pope;
- public worship in the vernacular, with the sacraments restricted to Baptism and the Lord's Supper;
- worship that emphasised preaching, reading the Bible and common prayers;
- an educated, preaching Ministry supported by Readers;
- authority in the church shared between elders (often lairds) and ministers; gathered in local Kirk Sessions, sometimes provincial Assemblies (later Presbyteries) and the General Assembly (in which the reformed nobility also originally sat);
- the discipline of a Christian life expected (and imposed where necessary) from all – not just the 'religious' or the clergy;
- a social programme including care for the poor and sick;
- an educational programme including improved universities and a school in each town.

The true preaching of the Word of God ... the right administration of the Sacraments of Christ Jesus ... and lastly, Ecclesiastical Discipline uprightly administered, as God's Word prescribes ... where ever these notes are seen ... there, beyond any doubt, is the true Kirk of Christ.
From the Scots' Confession of Faith: approved by Parliament at Edinburgh, 1560.

To implement this programme throughout Scotland, the General Assembly during the 1560s gave its authority to superintendents or commissioners – ministers with a bishop-like authority over a 'diocese'; those existing bishops who reformed and accepted the authority of the Assembly could and did receive such 'Commissions'.

In Orkney, Bishop Adam Bothwell conformed and attempted to reform the county. In 1570 he gave a defence of his actions in this period to the General Assembly:[14]

> When idolatry and superstition were suppressed, he suppressed the same also in his bounds, preached the Word, administered the Sacraments, planted Ministers in Orkney and Zetland, and gave stipends out of his rents to ministers, exhorters and readers, and (subsequently) when he was a Commissioner, visited all the Kirks of Orkney and Zetland twice, to the hazard of his life, in dangerous storms on the seas . . .

The seas were not the only hazards Bothwell had to face. The population of Orkney had little interest in favouring the Reformation and many preferred a religion sanctioned by tradition. The Bishop wrote this account to his friends south:[15]

> A great multitude of the commons met at the first Head Court after Yule. When they were all gathered, certain of my agents, sent for the purpose, enquired if they would consent to change the accepted mode of religion; which they refused. Notwithstanding that decision and rebuff, I closed the doors of my kirk [St Magnus] and have permitted no Mass to be said there since; which so irritated my opponents that, after they had sundry times required me to give way, at last gathered together in great number and brought a priest to a chapel who both celebrated Mass and conducted the marriage of certain couples in the old manner. This was done on Sunday last, which I could not have stopped without committing slaughter.

Support in Orkney for the Reformation might well have been curtailed by its sponsorship by the Protestant English, who were highly unpopular in the islands. Clashes over fishing grounds during the sixteenth century had led to full-scale naval conflict and a battle at Papdale as late as 13 August 1557 against a landing force that captured the Cathedral and bombarded the Castle of Kirkwall. Several hundred Englishmen were killed and the Admiral drowned.[16] Yet at least some of the Scottish Reforming faction advocated a full union with England in a united Protestant Britain. The Lords of the Congregation, in requesting military support from England, also spoke a royal marriage for 'the union of these twoo kyngdomes in one'.[17] The same navy that had invaded Orkney, two years later ensured the Protestant victory in Scotland.

Though public opinion may well have been against Reform, nevertheless such events as highly public protest do not happen without leadership. Identifying opponents of Bishop Adam Bothwell is, however, difficult at this distance. It was difficult for himself at the time. It is clear that the public meeting at the Headcourt refused to give its consent to church reform. To decline may have indicated committed support for the Catholic Church – or it might have meant a more limited refusal to share responsibility for an act which might later attract dangerous attention from a Catholic Queen. Besides, the practice of saying 'No' and waiting on events is not confined to the sixteenth century! Moreover, to give an initial refusal to a request can increase a bargaining position – and there were many who wished to bargain with the young bishop to their advantage. From his letters he obviously had some difficulty distinguishing between enemies to be bought off, and friends who needed their reward. Members of the important Orkney family of Sinclair came into both camps.[18]

Though the Earldom of Orkney was annexed to the Crown, the Sinclair descendants of the former Earls still held considerable power, whether as lairds or, as sometimes, exercising judicial power under the Crown. One of Bishop Bothwell's sponsors, Oliver Sinclair of Pitcairns, had held a lease of all the Crown's lands in Orkney at one stage; his local agent and sheriff depute was Edward Sinclair of Strome. From Bishop Robert Reid, Edward Sinclair and his wife had obtained a feu of bishopric lands in Scockness, Rousay; the charter's preamble asserting that the Bishop was motived by Sinclair's faithful support of him in the diocese of Orkney, 'in defence of Christen fayt and libertie of haly kirk'.[19] At an earlier stage a known friend to the Catholic Church, Sinclair of Strome may, therefore, have some loyalty to the policies of Robert Reid after the old bishop's death. Strome's sons, Henry and Robert, were certainly among Adam Bothwell's most open opponents between 1560 and 1561. A petition with 18-20 items was presented by them, rejecting the religious changes introduced by the bishop – and a band of their men forcibly occupied his palace at Birsay and threatened him with death. Perhaps seeing that dissent was in danger of becoming rebellion, Edward of Strome cooled down his family's hotheads:[20]

[he] withstood [them] calling him [Robert Sinclair] and the laity 'Fools that didn't know what they were doing'; and said that he 'Could not in any way consent to the Mass being celebrated.'

Adam Bothwell appears to have been 'set up' by, among others, Oliver Sinclair. It seems likely that his sponsors encouraged him to proceed with reform, while privately indicating to those of their kin ready to listen that a measure of opposition might be called for. The more difficulties he encountered, the more he would need their support – and the more lands and revenues of the bishopric would come their way. Oliver Sinclair obtained lands in Eday and later passed them on to his nephew, another Edward Sinclair. The passing of the lands of the bishopric into private hands was one of the most significant social effects of the Reformation.

With the decision of Sinclair of Strome not to oppose the abolition of the Mass, Adam Bothwell's Reformation in Orkney was free to proceed. The key task was to secure staff for Orkney's parishes. St Magnus Cathedral, of course, no longer needed a team of its own; the Reformed Church needed not cathedrals but all the parish ministers it could find, and besides, the concept of non-parochial ministers was unacceptable in principle (though superintendents were unavoidable in the early years). The requirement to preach, however, meant that a level of education was needed; and that meant, in turn, that a level of stipend was needed to attract the educated. All this took time; meanwhile, before ministers were easily available and affordable, parishes were served in groups, as they had been before 1560, with a visiting minister in charge, and local people appointed as readers. Readers literally read the Bible passages and if necessary the Prayers as well, whether their own or from the English Prayer Book or the Genevan Book of Common Order. Only with the services of readers could public worship be maintained in every parish in the first decades of the Reformation.

The Protestant reformers in Scotland had believed they were reforming the existing church, not starting a new one. They acknowledged, for example, baptism according to Catholic rites as a true Christian baptism. They expected the people of Scotland to be in membership of the reformed church; they expected to retain possession of the buildings – churches and manses – and of the income of the church in Scotland. They looked, therefore, to pay their ministry through the compulsory tithe. What about, however, those Catholic clergy who were legally entitled to the tithe and had no wish to serve a Protestant church? Successive governments over the years devised a variety of compromise arrangements. During the 1560s all existing Catholic clergy kept two thirds of their legal income as a pension, whether they worked or not. The Crown collected the other third of the income of all parish and cathedral benefices, taking responsibility for paying the Protestant ministry and using some of this revenue for its own purposes. If a priest conformed and served the reformed church, however, he kept for himself both the two-thirds and the third. As the Catholic clergy died, then the new church was entitled to reclaim the whole of the revenue of parish and cathedral chapter posts for its ministers.

In his article on 'Sixteenth Century Reform', Duncan Shaw considered that 'almost all of the parishes in Orkney' had the services of minister, reader or exhorter[21] by 1567. Together with the late Professor Gordon Donaldson, he considered this a mark of the success of Adam Bothwell's Reformation of Orkney.[22] But this judgment very much depends both on what is considered to be a 'parish' and on what 'services' a reformed congregation ought to expect of its ministry. Certainly the three parishes of Sanday, the two parishes of Westray, Papay and North Ronaldsay had 'the services of a minister': all seven of them were allocated as one charge to the same minister, Mr Annand, assisted by two readers. This was not abundant provision of ministry and can hardly even be described as adequate. A substantial number of parishes had no minister allocated at all and were served by readers, who could not preach: Shapinsay, Evie, Rendall, Hoy and Walls, Flotta, South Ronaldsay's two parishes and Burray. At Holm, Nicol Craigie was exhorter and there was no minister. It seems that in 1567 Orkney had eight reformed ministers, twelve readers and two exhorters. Certainly elsewhere in Scotland there are known to have been some discrepancies between what happened on the ground and what was recorded in national records. In this case, the suspicion is that ministers are named who did not in fact serve. Two of the earliest ministers, Mr Francis Bothwell (Stronsay and Eday) and Mr Thomas Beanston (Rousay and Egilsay), vanished from Orkney as Bishop Adam Bothwell left the diocese.[23] By 1574 only four of the ministers were left of the ministry of the years immediately after the Reformation: Mr James Annand, Mr Jerome Tulloch, Thomas Stevenson and Mr Gilbert Foulsie. Additionally, Thomas Rattray, a former priest who had become a reader in South Ronaldsay had been promoted to be minister of Shapinsay.

The following table is a partial transcription of the key document for the ministry in Orkney in 1567-70. It was designed in 1567 in order to record the sums due to the reformed clergy, and it indicated how much they were to have in cash from the Thirds of Benefices collected by the Crown, and how much they were entitled to keep from benefices they held themselves (i.e. their own third and the two-thirds as well, of course!). The document was maintained until 1570, with alterations and deletions as people moved or died. The secretaries have made errors, with some double-entries of both people and places. Probably the clerks in Edinburgh had little knowledge of the geography of Orkney. This version of the document has modernised names and leaves out the actual sums of money involved – though that would, no doubt, have been of most interest to the people involved in the 1560s![24]

Register of Ministers, Exhorters and Readers: Diocese of Orkney

Parish	Officebearer	Revenues allocated
f.73r Kirkwall	Mr Gilbert Foulsie, Minister	Third of his Vicarages of Birsay/Harray; Prebend of St John Altarage of St Ola and more since Nov.70.
St Ola	John Sadler, Reader	Third of Vicarage of St Ola
St Andrews }	Mr Donald Bruce, Minister	
Deerness } *[on top of erasure]*	Archibald Reid, Reader look after	Third of Vicarages of Holm and Deerness
Deerness *[erased]*	Gavin Watt, Reader	Third of his Vicarage-pensionary
	Archibald Reid, Reader	Third of Vicarages of Holm and Deerness, Nov.68 translated to Evie, Nov.70.
Holm Nov.68	Nicol Craigie, Exhorter	Third of Vicarage
Firth, } Orphir } Stenness }	Thomas Stevenson, Minister	Third of Subdeanery and more since Nov.69

Holm } Deerness }	John Stewart, Reader	Third of his Vicarage at Nov. 70 Third of Vicar-pensioner of Deerness, same time.
f.73v Birsay } Harray }	Mr Donald Walker, Minister Robert Stewart, Reader	Third of his Vicarage-pensionary and more since Nov. 70
~~Sanct Columbs~~ Stromness } Sandwick } Graemsay }	Mr Jerome Tulloch, Minister William Smith, Reader	Subchanter, with his Third allowed Third of Vicarage-pensionary since Nov. 67 and more since Nov. 68
St Ronaldsay } died Nov. 70 Burray }	Duncan Ramsay, Reader Edward Ingster, Reader	Thirds of Vicarage-pensionary and in his room .. Third of Vicarage-pensionary and more since Nov. 70
Walls } Hoy } Flotta } Faray }	Mr William Moodie, Minister John Molyson, Reader Thomas Fleming, Reader	Dues of the Common Kirk, Nov. 70 Third of Vicarage-pensionary Third of his Vicarage-pensionary and more since Nov. 70
~~Eynhallow~~ Rousay } Egilsay } Wyre } Eynhallow }	Laurence Young, Exhorter	Third of Vicarage-pensionary more since Nov. 68
f.74r Westray } look after } Papa Westray }	Mr James Annand, Minister William Brown, Reader	Thirds of Vicarages of Crosskirk and Sanday Third of his Vicarage-pensionary
Shapinsay	Thomas Rattray, Reader	Third of the Vicarage
Stromness		
Sandwick		
look before at Holm	John Stewart, Reader translated to Holm/Deerness, since Nov. 70	Third of Vicarage-pensionary
Evie } Rendall } Gairsay }	Archibald Reid, Reader in his room, Third of Vicarage-pensionary more since 70	
f.74v Hoy Flotta		
Sanday North Ronaldsay }	Mr James Annand, Minister Thomas Tailor, Reader,	Third of Parsonage of Marykirk in Sanday Vicarages of Sanday and North Ronaldsay Nov. 68 with Third of Vicarage-pensionary Westray
Rousay Egilsay Wyre		
f.75r Stronsay } Eday } PapaStronsay }	Mr James Maxwell, Reader	Third of his benefices, extending to £20, Nov. 69

A certain amount is known (and more can be guessed) about the first reformed ministry of Orkney. Francis Bothwell was a former friar who arrived in Orkney as minister at Stronsay with his kinsman the bishop and left with him before 1567. Gilbert Foulsie, a priest and former monk, was Bothwell's secretary: first appointed by him to a junior canonry and then as Archdeacon. James Annand had already been a junior canon in the Cathedral before 1560. He was promoted by Bothwell to the lucrative post of Chancellor. Though the spiritual responsibilities of the Dignitaries of the Chapter had ended, the business side of its affairs continued – and so did their income from tithes, rents, legacies etc. Annand became minister responsible for the whole of Westray, Papay, Sanday and North Ronaldsay, assisted by readers for each island. Professor Gordon Donaldson suggested Annand was 'quite the most reliable' of the clergy Bishop Bothwell found in office[25] – though it seems likely his parishioners might not have agreed. The suspicion must be that, as a senior clergyman, Annand continued the pre-Reformation practice of not being resident in his parish(es).

Of the pre-Reformation senior clergy, it took the Provost, Mr Alexander Dick, until 1574 before he consented to serve as minister for the lands that provided his stipend – South Ronaldsay and Burray. In 1567, he had been accused in the General Assembly of saying Mass and being an enemy of religion. The ancient image of St Peter, venerated in South Ronaldsay, remained there until 1643, when Presbytery ordered it to be burnt.[26] Alexander Dick was the only one of the dignitaries to conform to the Reformation. Mr Magnus Halcro, Chantor of the Cathedral, did not serve the new church; he was in fact accused by it of adultery.[27] It took until 1585 before a Halcro, Mr Ninian, appeared as minister at Rousay, Egilsay and Wyre. The Subdean, Mr Peter Houston, and the Subchanter, Magnus Strang, also declined to serve; both dying only a few years after 1560, they may have been already ill or elderly as well as disinclined to assist the reformed church. Of the minor prebends, Mr William Pierson, Holy Cross canon, obtained his revenues from the church of that name on Sanday. He was one of the regular notaries for contracts made in Kirkwall, and became minister at St Andrews, Deerness and Holm in 1574. Otherwise, Mr James Maxwell, who held the Vicarage of Stronsay and was St Katherine's Stouk Chaplain, was the only other canon to join James Annand in following the lead of Bishop Adam Bothwell by accepting office in the reformed Church. The following table italicises those of the Chapter who conformed and who served in the new Church – and when.[28]

Dignitaries

Provost	*Mr Alexander Dick*	*Conformed in 1574*
Archdeacon	Vacant in 1561 when Mr Gilbert Foulsie was appointed	
Precentor	Mr Magnus Halcro	did not serve
Chancellor	Vacant in 1561 when Mr James Annand was appointed	
Treasurer	Vacant in 1561 when Mr Francis Bothwell was appointed	
Subdean	Mr Peter Houston	did not serve
Subchanter	Magnus Strang	did not serve

Minor canons

Holy Cross	*Mr William Pierson*	*Conformed in 1574*
St Magnus	Vacant in 1561 when Robert Cheyne was appointed	
St John	*Mr James Annand*	*Conformed immediately and promoted*
Woodwick	John Anderson	did not serve
St Laurence	(Mr James Annand held together with St John)	
St Katherine	*Mr James Maxwell*	*Conformed immediately*
St Duthac	Mr John Houston	did not serve

On Stronsay, the Vicar, Mr James Maxwell, had been in post since 1541. He immediately conformed to the new church, serving until 1576. In 1571, a charter records that marriage contracts were agreed between his daughters Margaret and Janet and sons of David Sinclair of Hunto; the contract specified that the ceremonies should be church services.[29] Priests of the Catholic Church were officially celibate: reformed ministers could lawfully enjoy family life. Gilbert Foulsie, minister at Kirkwall and Birsay with Harray married Elizabeth Kinnaird, and set up house in the Archdeacon's Manse opposite the Cathedral; their crests and motto still remain over the gateway to what is now Tankerness House. *'Without the Lord's protection our children will live in vain and ourselves be but slaves'*.[30] The united parish of Birsay and Harray, however, had not obtained a minister of its own by 1590. Perhaps the minister attended when the Earl was resident in Birsay; otherwise, Robert Stewart no doubt conducted worship as reader in the joint country parish.

It was to be expected that the Cathedral clergy would be reluctant to serve in the new church. Quite apart from doctrinal issues, there had been little demand on them to conduct worship before 1560 and they could not be said to have had a pastoral ministry. Decision-makers and administrators as well as celebrants of the Mass, they probably felt quite unsuited to the new role of preacher and pastor. The parish clergy, however, were rather more ready to become Protestant ministers. The Vicars of Stronsay (Mr James Maxwell), South Ronaldsay (Duncan Ramsay) and Holm (Nicol Craigie) all decided to serve in the new church soon after 1560. Of the Vicars-Pensioner (those who served parishes where vicarages were appropriated, or who shared duties with, or substituted for, a Vicar) Mr John Duncanson (Stromness) almost certainly and probably William Brown (Westray), Laurence Young (Rousay), Thomas Rattray (South Ronaldsay), John Malison (Flotta), David Anderson (Evie/Rendall) and Gavin Watt (Deerness/St Andrews) may all have held office before 1560 and conformed thereafter. Some of the reformers must have been young men when first appointed – Laurence Young, Jerome Tulloch, Thomas Rattray and William Peirson all served the new church for over thirty years. James and Jerome Tulloch may well have come from an Orcadian family as may Mr John Houston (or was it Hourston?) and Edward Ingster. In general, it seems that Bishop Adam Bothwell was well content to appoint existing clergy to serve their parishes as ministers or readers where they were able and willing. He promoted a few key younger men; he brought with him a few allies.

Adam Bothwell seems to have been a conscientious bishop of Orkney, though described by his descendent Mark Napier as 'boring', prone to writing sound spiritual advice in family letters to female relatives. He seems to have been able to generate little local spiritual enthusiasm for his policies, winning over next to none of the Chapter of his Cathedral. Neither did he have much political influence of his own in Edinburgh; yet he controlled a bishopric with substantial lands and income. These he was forced to part with: by Oliver Sinclair of Pitcairns; by another patron, a lawyer powerful at court: Bellenden of Auchnoule, Justice-

Clerk; and by his brother-in-law the adventurer Gilbert Balfour, who built Noltland Castle, on Westray, which still stands as a testimony to the need he felt for protection and defence. In 1570, having granted to these and others much of the income of the bishopric, Adam Bothwell was compelled to exchange the remaining revenues, lands and powers of his post with Lord Robert Stewart, Abbot of Holyroodhouse and step-brother to Queen Mary. Bishop Bothwell does not appear to have been in Orkney after 1567. Lord Robert also became Earl of Orkney, thus controlling the lands, revenues and patronage of both the Crown and the Bishopric. He came north to exercise his powers in person as a sort of Stewart throw-back to the days of the Norse warrior-Earls.[31]

To replace Bishop Bothwell, the General Assembly appointed as Commissioner in Orkney, Mr James Annand; and as Commissioner in Shetland, Gilbert Foulsie. The secular rule of the Stewart earls in Orkney is a long and troublesome story, but the commissioner-ministers seem to have continued the undemanding policies begun by the reforming Bishop Bothwell and with rather better success. Robert Stewart's half-brother James, Earl of Moray, sometime Regent of Scotland, was a convinced Protestant. The Earl of Orkney does seem to have accommodated in religious matters to the murdered Regent's lead, though his new Palace at Birsay was apparently adorned in traditional style with Biblical scenes and texts.[32] In the early 1580s he contemplated having his heir Patrick educated in Catholic France 'in respect of their religion' – but a College in Protestant England was also in his mind and nothing came of either suggestion.[33] Earl Robert's interests seem to have lain less in theology and more in obtaining tacks or feus of Church lands or tithes. By these contracts, clergy gave a lease of their revenues for a set annual sum and the 'tenant' then made whatever profit he could from raising the tithe for himself. In an era of inflation, the annual sum paid under contract lost value, and the tenant's profits increased. Earl Robert's conflict with Mr James Maxwell was probably because as Vicar of Stronsay Maxwell also held the quite extensive lands of the Cathedral Chaplaincy of St Katherine's Stouk.[34]

As might be expected in an era when society operated via the patronage of the powerful, various of the new ministry appear to have been associated with and promoted by those who held power in Orkney. John Stewart first occurs as Reader at Evie and Rendall in 1567, the year Lord Robert Stewart arrived in Orkney. He was moved to Holm, Deerness and St Andrews in 1570 and by 1576 had the Curates' Chamber and a cellar in the 'New Wirk' in Kirkwall as reader at the Cathedral. Meanwhile another Robert Stewart had obtained a vicarage at Birsay and Harray in 1567 and was recorded as reader there to 1590. In 1576 he also served as Clerk to the Baillie Court at Harray. A young man who presumably came to Orkney with his namesake and patron, this Robert Stewart lived to 1633 and was buried at Holm.[35] On the other hand, the Henderson brothers, Cuthbert and William, seem to have been associated with the business affairs of Bellenden of Auchnoule, patron first to Bishop Bothwell and then to Patrick Bellenden. William was officially minister at Stronsay and Eday in 1580. By 1585 he had been succeeded by Cuthbert, who had previously been reader at Rousay. The ministerial post brought with it the dignity, lands and revenues of Treasurer of the Cathedral, to which was annexed the parsonage assets of North Ronaldsay. The Hendersons went on to acquire Holland in North Ronaldsay for themselves.[36]

If Earl Robert managed to obtain the minor post of reader for at least two of his kin, he ran in trouble when attempting to influence the appointment of senior ministers. In 1587 he was accused in Parliament of illegally acting as patron for the parishes connected to the major Cathedral dignitaries – the Provost, Chancellor, Archdeacon and Chanter. The national Register of ministers in post shows that Mr Alex Cheyne, the minister of Sanday and North Ronaldsay, was deleted from the lists in 1586 and one James Stewart added; the parishes formed part of the Chancellor's benefice. The Earl's kinsman's name was, however, also deleted and Mr James Cook was finally admitted to the charge. In South Ronaldsay and Burray (the Provost's charge) one Alexander Callender is listed as minister 1585-1588. An Andrew Callender had attended the earl in his younger days and held lands from him in the south. By 1590, South Ronaldsay and Burray was in the hands of a local minister, Mr Ninian Halcro, who had transferred from Rousay. Evidence for the Earl's tampering with appointments to the parishes and revenues of the Archdeacon and Chanter is less obvious in the record. Birsay and Harray (the archdeaconry) remained officially vacant between 1585 and 1590; it may be that the Earl had put his own man in place without informing the national secretariat at all. Harry

Colville, minister at parishes connected to the Chanter's benefice, Orphir, Stenness, Firth, has no known connection with the Earl and his arrival in Orkney was earlier, in 1580.[37]

The reformed church, at least superficially, achieved many of its objectives in Orkney. A parish ministry, increasingly staffed by resident ministers, led Sunday worship in the reformed manner. The resources of the church (at least, those left to the church) went to the parish ministry and not to St Magnus and its staff. The Cathedral was gradually emptied of its various chaplaincies and altars. The choir was screened off to provide a relatively sheltered area for the congregation, and pews and galleries were erected.[38] The Mass was outlawed. Eventually we also hear of trials for witchcraft, as that unhappy fashion swept Scotland.[39] The number of ministers in the county gradually increased, from six in 1567 to thirteen in 1590, of whom seven were graduates. At the same time, their charges were reduced in size to (possibly) pastorally manageable proportions. James Annand's impossible charge of North Ronaldsay, Sanday, Papay and Westray was split in two. Jerome Tulloch's equally impossible linkage of Stromness, Sandwick, Rousay, Egilsay and Wyre lasted most of the 1570s. By 1580, it was also split on a Mainland/islands basis. Similarly, the 1570s grouping of Evie, Firth, Rendall, Orphir and Stenness under one minister was broken into two in 1580 – Firth went with Orphir and Stenness, and Evie and Rendall had Eynhallow added to them.[40]

During the 1570s, the Kirk nationally was attempting to strengthen its parish ministry. From 1574, official policy under Regent Morton was to extend the system of grouping parishes in threes or fours, so that each had a reader of its own with a minister leading the team. Some opposed this policy at the time, on the grounds that (though it was a practical use of available funds) it did not provide a proper ministry, one both pastorally involved and preaching regularly. The argument was best put by John Davidson, of St Leonard's College, St Andrews:[41]

> And first, I said this ordour makis
> Far greiter burdingis on mennis bakis
> Be laid, nor thay dow for to beir,
> As I sall schortly let zow heir;

For ane man cannot satisfie
For to do four mennis dewtle.

Bot quhen ane man hes vnder cure
Sa mony thousandis, riche and pure,
Scarsly will he ken ilkane,
Quhen twentie zeiris at cum and gane.

Besides preaching, Davidson held that a minister's duties included visiting:

To veseit, comfort seik and pure;
And that into particulair,
As it salbe found necessair:

All in all, he considered that 'four parishes to one minister' would deprive Scotland of the Gospel:

It will defraude syne, secundlie,
The present age of this Countrie
Of the maist hailsum word of lyfe.

Davidson's argument was that one man cannot do the duty of four; for the preacher should also be a pastor, and 'sould not the pastour knaw his scheip'. His poetry of 1574 describes the ideal preaching, visiting, pastoral ministry that came to dominate the Presbyterian vision of ministry. The next generation of the Kirk's leadership increasingly tried to separate the groupings of parishes to provide one graduate minister to one parish, phasing out the readers. In Orkney, however, long-standing unions like Harray and Birsay or Stromness and Sandwick remained unaffected by the new national policy, which was associated with the more radical Presbyterian faction of Andrew Melville. Continuity rather than radical change was the hallmark of Orkney's Reformation.

Though the structures of the Reformed Faith in Orkney gradually grew stronger, nevertheless for decades and more the folk of the county continued with traditions from the Catholic era: remembering the traditional feast-days of their parish's patron-saint, visiting the ancient ruins of chapels. The first 'tourist' to leave a report of his visit to Orkney, Jo. Ben, writing in the sixteenth century, had commented of the people of North Ronaldsay:[42] '*The people are very ignorant of divine discourse, because they are seldom or ever taught.*'

Similarly, of the island of Stronsay he wrote that '*They also greatly believe in fairies*' and described the creature known in Orkney folklore as a 'trow'. Shapinsay, too, came in for his criticism: '*The people inhabiting this island are very ignorant: they worship fairies and other wicked things.*'

In 1609, Earl Patrick was to defend a harsh sentence against an Orcadian male witch on the grounds that the people[43] '*wald all have becommit witchis and warlockis for the people ar naturally inclynit thairto.*'

A further hundred years on, and another visitor, Rev. John Brand, wrote of the veneration for the ancient chapels of St Tredwell (Westray) and Marykirk (South Ronaldsay) and the vows made at them, and of the continuing practice of observing the traditional saints' days. Communities had their own 'charmers', who were reputed to stop bleeding by reciting a charm, even at a distance. Other charms were used at childbirth, when animals were ill, or for success in fishing. Brand purported to be shocked at observing the continuing life of the Middle Ages in 1701, for safety putting all such customs in the category of 'heathenish and Popish rites'. He also cautioned that he was not accusing 'the generality of Orkney' but only the 'foolish and silly', lacking education.[44]

> for Ignorance of the Principles of our Holy Religion, doth greatly prevail among the Commonalty, so that one of their Ministers, not without some concern and grief for the same, told me, Not one of a hundred in some of their Parishes can read. How this comes to pass, that the people should be so grossly Ignorant I shall not undertake to determine, it is commonly imputed to their want of Schools, through the Country, which indeed I will not say but is one great cause thereof . . .

Education means the provision of schools – and that means the upkeep of buildings and the payment of teachers. The lack of enthusiasm for reformed ideals among Orkney's political classes – or, alternatively, their pursuit of income and lands – seems to have resulted in a general failure for decades after 1560 to find resources for education. The ideals of the national educational programme of 1560 were not, however, wholly overlooked in Orkney. On 1 November 1633, the minister of South Ronaldsay and the laird, Hugh Halcro, younger, of that ilk, contracted with Andrew Strang that he should read the due chapter of the Bible and lead prayer in the Peter and Lady Kirks every alternate Sunday; and also instruct the children of South Ronaldsay to read and write.[45] There is no evidence for other rural schools.[46] Kirkwall, of course, had its Grammar School, whose teacher was associated with the Cathedral and paid from tithe belonging to the former prebend of St Peter. Mr John Houston (Hourston?), a priest before the Reformation, signed himself as Schoolmaster in 1554, at which time the prefix 'Mr' stood for 'Magister' or the university degree MA. In 1576, he obtained the living of the vicar pensioner of the parish of St Andrews, with its manse and glebe, while continuing to hold the Cathedral prebend of St Peter. By 1578, he called himself the 'Schoolmaster of the town of Kirkwall'.[47]

Apart from necessary local co-operation between laird and minister, it is difficult to find non-ministerial leaders of the reformed church in Orkney in the Reformation period. In Scotland, it had been largely devout, converted lairds and elders who led the way before 1560 and then became elders and leaders of the church thereafter. In Orkney, such evidence of enthusiasm for the new ways seems non-existent. On the contrary, in 1588, the General Assembly chose to appoint a Ross-shire minister to visit Orkney, considering the county a place 'where the jesuits and papists cheflie resort'. The county converted because it had to: the Bishop and the Stewart Earls between them had sufficient secular clout to enforce national policies, though the earls lack credibility as sponsors of the church's ideals. Besides, the concept of purgatory seems to have lost plausibility before 1560 and lacking that as an element of faith, the traditional value of the Mass had vanished, even though Orcadians instinctively preferred ceremonies hallowed by tradition.

The career of Mr William Moodie makes a useful example of one type of new minister in Orkney. A graduate, he was the Crown's Chamberlain in Orkney by 1554, when Kirkwall Castle and Orkney were held for the Crown by a Frenchman on behalf of the French princess, Regent of Scotland, Mary of Guise. Indeed, he held a commission from the Regent in 1551 to hear complaints against the then governor of the bishopric lands. Moodie's family appear to have been tenants in Hoy. Mr William had studied at St Andrews *c*.1538. In 1555,he accompanied Adam Bothwell on his first known visit to the islands. A figure, then, of some stature in Orkney, in company with Sinclair of Strome he was attacked in the Cathedral in 1561 by a group including Mr Magnus Halcro. When in 1564 his son Adam married one Grizel Stewart, Lord (later Earl) Robert Stewart granted him lands, and he gained further lands from Magnus Halcro, perhaps in a mutual settlement, in 1565. By 1568, in alliance with those who had gained Orcadian lands from Bishop Bothwell, Patrick Bellenden and Gilbert Balfour, he was said to be plotting with them to use force to keep Lord Robert out of Orkney. A fight in the Cathedral between men at arms of the various parties led to some deaths. William Moodie, however, came out of the turmoil of the Reformation period as laird of Breckness and then of Melsetter. From 1570 to 1590, he also served the new Kirk as minister for the parish in which his lands lay: Hoy and Walls (with Flotta and Graemsay also in the charge). Somehow always on the winning side, he was one of those commissioned in 1577 to hear the complaints of the people of Shetland against Lord Robert's agent there, Bruce of Cultmalindie.[48]

Orkney's nineteenth century Church Historian, Rev. J.B. Craven, accepted the utility of the Orkney Reformation and thought little of the first reformed ministers of the church.[49]

> And what are we to think of all these old priests who appear to have conformed so easily to the new order of things? . . . The writer has often thought over the matter, and has reluctantly come to the conclusion that all real religion – religion affecting life and heart – was well-nigh banished from the country. The state of the laity was deplorable; ignorance amongst the clergy was equally rife . . . As to the character and ability of the Orkney clergy of the first generation after the Reformation, we do not know much, and what we do know does not give us a very high opinion of their knowledge or sincerity . . . It is, however, probable that the progress and completion of the Reformation in Orkney was due more to

its present applicability to men's needs than to the high character of those who brought it to its conclusion.

What has been discovered since 1900 does not lead to a more generous conclusion. Peter D. Anderson's book on Earl Patrick Stewart, though its focus is entirely political, does on occasion mention the ministry in passing. We learn, therefore, that Thomas Swinton, minister in Kirkwall, was not only the minister for the Cathedral, but also Earl Patrick's 'notary and henchman'. Swinton had been one of those required to give surety to the Crown for keeping the peace in 1597.[50] Harry Colville, minister at Orphir, Stenness and Firth, was yet more notorious. As minister he held the Subdean's benefice, and additionally had been appointed to the earldom post of Chamberlain of Orkney. In an attempt to find evidence against Patrick's brother and rival John, Colville led the prosecution against Thomas Paplay and Alison Balfour, accused of plotting Patrick's death by poison. The minister supervised the questioning of the suspects by torture – which was extended to Balfour's husband, son and seven-year old daughter. Followers of John Stewart successfully murdered Colville in 1596.[51]

Episcopalian and Presbyterian – aftermath of Reformation

From 1560, the Church's ministers were paid (like their Catholic predecessors), directly or indirectly by the compulsory tithe – a tax on the produce of the land. Each parish was intended to have its own Kirk Session, whose eldership sought to maintain order in the church and morality in society. The voluntary offerings of the congregations supplied Poor Funds, which the Sessions disbursed as they thought fit to those in need – this was often the only possible source provided by society for relief for the poor. Where schools existed, the Sessions also came to examine, appoint and authorise the local schoolmasters. The national Church, then, played a crucial role in society, its ministers well-educated and often fairly well off. It had a legal title to, and administered, a substantial part of the wealth of Scotland. Who governed the church and who benefited from its wealth were questions of political importance. Besides, the bishops of Orkney, as well as enjoying the tithe of a good many parishes, had also been substantial landlords in their own right. The bishop for the time was probably the wealthiest man in the county, and besides his spiritual authority, enjoyed the considerable legal powers that lairds held under the feudal system.

Though the General Assembly during the 1570s came to a theology that rejected the need for bishops, the Scottish bishops remained an essential part of the Scottish Parliament and were useful agents of royal government. A further series of compromises between 1586 and 1592 stripped the bishops of their secular lands (which were annexed to the Crown) but retained the men and their office as administrators of the church, permanent chairmen of the Presbyteries, as well as being the ministers of the congregations of their cathedrals. The Stuart kings, however, continued (when politically able so to do) to foster a church in which the bishops they nominated would have all their traditional powers, maintaining a continuity of ordination held by some to be an essential link with the days of the apostles, and acting as agents of the supremacy in the church of a divinely-anointed monarch.

In Orkney, Bishop James Law (appointed 1605) was a convinced Episcopalian, arguing in the Glasgow General Assembly of 1610 for the rightness of episcopal government within the Christian Church. He insisted that all existing ministers in Orkney obtain from him new licence to fulfil their functions, thus restoring the ancient Catholic principle of ministry flowing from a bishop whose own consecration was in succession to the apostle Peter. Besides his ecclesiastical powers, Law also came to serve as King James' Commissioner, Sheriff and Justice-Depute in Orkney, exercising a formidable array of authority. Indeed, his appointment, on the king's own initiative, was intended to serve at least two ends. Law was a royal agent to restore regular government in the Northern Isles at a time when Earl Patrick's personal affairs were bringing the two counties into turmoil; as a bishop, he was also part of the king's policy to restore full episcopacy in the Church.[52]

At the downfall of the last Stewart Earl, Patrick (beheaded for treason in 1615), Law was able to agree a settlement with the Crown to separate and clarify which lands and which revenues belonged to the Crown (i.e. the former earldom) and which to the bishopric. From the Charter of 1614 the Crown was the clear winner in financial terms, but the administrative gain was also substantial. Through the centuries since 995, both earldom and bishopric had gained lands and revenues on a geographically random basis throughout Orkney; and indeed, in Caithness and Shetland. The turmoil produced by the Reformation and the Stewart Earls had made a confused situation worse. In 1614, however, the Orkney diocese surrendered all its lands to the Crown, and in exchange was granted possessions strictly limited to distinct parishes. From 1614, Orkney's parishes could be described as either belonging to the earldom or to the bishopric. The bishop's authority was supreme in both ecclesiastical and civil matters in his parishes; he appointed his own sheriffs, held his own courts. The county's ministers obtained clear title to revenues they could rely on.

For Law's role in restoring a legal government in Orkney after the turmoil of Earl Patrick's years and the forlorn rising of his son Robert, and equally for his success in restoring a fully episcopal church here, Rev. J. Craven concludes:[53]

> Perhaps at some future time it will be more fully realised than at present that he had a better title than any other merely human person to be called 'The Saviour of Orkney'.

Certainly an able and committed man, James Law's episcopate lasted nine years to 1615, when he was promoted to be Archbishop of Glasgow. Whether he should be known as 'the Saviour of Orkney' is another matter. He played a large part in engineering the return to the Crown of the Earldom and the consequent abolition of Orkney law. The agents he appointed for collecting taxes were even more hated than those of the Earl. His role in jointly directing the Crown's military expedition to besiege and bombard the Castle of Kirkwall when it was garrisoned by Robert Stewart in 1614 has a mediaeval feel to it, though he personally did not fight. A chief agent of royal government, policies, politics and justice, with courts held and taxes collected in his name, Bishop James Law was certainly the key representative in Orkney of King James VI during his episcopate.[54] A later generation would consider that the separate roles of minister of Christ and minister of the Crown should not be so confused.

In 1627, under Law's successor, Bishop George Graham, a Royal

Commission took evidence in Orkney on the kirk's ministry to the parishes, and on how it was financed. The quality of the replies varied, but they show some of the concerns typical of the Scottish Church after the Reformation.[55]

The minister of Hoy and Walls, with two elders, wrote:

> Within the Parish of Hoy are 338 communicants. Within the Parish of Walls are 453 communicants. The Kirk of Hoy is united to the Kirk of Walls . . . The distance between the two kirks is 14 miles of moss and mount, with great waters in the way, in such sort that it is not possible for one minister to travel between the two kirks and serve the cure, especially in winter; for of the foresaid 14 miles there are 6 miles of wilderness, wherein are several great waters, neither is there any house by the way. The inhabitants of Gramsay [Graemsay] have ever been in use to come to the Parish Kirk of Hoy to hear the Word and receive the Sacraments. Flotta is an isle lying in the sea north-east from the Kirk of Walls, and [the inhabitants thereof are] in use to come there for hearing the Word etc. There is neither a school nor any foundation nor funds for a school in either of these two parishes with the adjacent isles. A school is necessary if it could be maintained, especially in Walls. We do not know of any provision that can be made for a school for the present. Neither are there any funds for a hospice in any of these parishes . . .[56]

The minister of Shapinsay wrote:

> The parish is not united to any other parish, but is of itself, being one Kirk, which serves the people thereof. No school in the parish, nor never was; because the people are poor labourers of the ground, and therefore are content their bairns be brought up to labour with them. No hospital in the parish, nor never was. The communicants are 250 persons.

The minister of Stromness wrote:

> First, anent the number of communicants, we have tested that there are four hundred and four score communicants, and sundry young people who shortly will be ready to take communion. The Kirk of Stromness is a distinct and individual kirk by itself, and no way is united nor can be easily united, for there are five miles distant between the Kirk of Stromness and the Kirk of Sandwick, very evil way: muirs, mosses and

burns; neither can the parishioners of the one parish resort to the other, but one minister has, and has had, the charge of both Kirks these many years past. There is no school in the parish nor foundation for a school, but great necessity of a school, for many youths yet want education.

These examples from the Royal Commission of 1627 show a church which emphasised:

- 'hearing the Word' and 'receiving the Sacraments' as the heart of a spiritual life;
- an ideal of general education – realised imperfectly or not at all;
- a continuation of the pre-Reformation practice of one minister serving several parishes;
- the instruction and preparation of communicants: the church gathered at the Lord's Supper;
- a general shortage of income to fund the work of the church.

Such concerns show the continuing pastoral task of the ministry, a task that went on whether Presbytery or Bishop was governing the church. As to its worship, this too continued, with some modifications according to the prevailing state of the struggle between Episcopalian and Presbyterian. One of the key dividing issues was whether it was right or not to kneel to receive communion. This had been the ancient Catholic practice, and for some was associated with the Catholic concept that the elements of bread and wine, on consecration, took on the virtues of the real body and blood of Jesus. Kneeling, then, could seen as veneration or worship of the elements to be received. Protestants following Calvin, however, insisted that the bread and wine remained bread and wine, that Christ's presence in the Supper was not physical but spiritual, understood through faith; and that worship addressed to things of this world was idolatry. John Knox had written that at the Lord's Supper, all (including the presiding minister) should dress alike and as equals sit around the table. His heirs in the Scottish ministry considered that any idea of worshipping the elements was blasphemous – and so declined to kneel, even when commanded so to do by the King. James Law, as Archbishop of Glasgow, excluded from his church those who refused to kneel; no doubt he had also insisted on the older forms while in Orkney.

Orkney's church was swept along by the tide of political and ecclesiastical turmoil that engulfed all of Britain during the reign of Charles I. The Civil War; Cromwell's conquest of Scotland and Ireland; the Covenanting Movement; the Restoration of Charles II, succeeded by his brother James – 1638-1690 was a period of political, military and religious strife. When possible, these Stuart Kings enforced Episcopal rule over the Scottish Church. Some ministers who refused to accept the authority of bishops were banished – to Orkney! For example, the minister of Colvend, Dumfriesshire, was banished to North Ronaldsay, from where he wrote:[57]

> The poor inhabitants, so many as I have yet seen, have received me with much joy (as I apprehend). I intend, if the Lord will, to preach Christ to them next Lord's day without the least mixture of any thing that may smell of sedition or rebellion. If I be further troubled for it, I resolve to suffer further wt. meekness and patience.

In southern Scotland some rose in rebellion against the episcopal policies of Charles II. These Covenanters were defeated at Bothwell

The Covenanters' Memorial, Deerness, Orkney

Bridge (1679). Some, being transported to America, were drowned when the prison ship *The Crown* foundered off Deerness, where a later generation erected a Monument to them. Even at the time, it seems that there was some sympathy in Orkney for those loyal to the Covenant – it is thought that some escaped from the wreck and were hidden by the local people.[58]

In 1689 the revolution against James VII & II that brought William of Orange to the thrones of both Scotland and England returned the Presbyterian system to the kirk. After 1690, Orkney's parish ministry was to be provided by the nationally-established Presbyterian Church of Scotland.

Not all in Orkney accepted the restoration of Presbytery, however. Rev. John Wilson, minister of the First Charge at St Magnus, remained a convinced Episcopalian and was deprived of his post. An illegal Episcopalian congregation continued to meet even when he left the county. The story of the strife between Kirkwall's Episcopalian and Presbyterian congregations is told by B.H. Hossack in his *Kirkwall in the Orkneys*. An important family of lairds, the Baikies of Tankerness, made 'the Chaplains' Chambers' – part of the pre-Reformation patrimony of the kirk and situated on Broad Street – available as a 'Meeting House' for the Episcopalians. A priest, James Lyon, was secured to conduct worship – and even marriages, for old Scottish law required only witnesses to a couple's mutual promises. The magistrates and Town Council effectively prevented the Presbytery from suppressing this illegal competitor. Hossack commented:

> The little congregation in the Meeting House, in spite of all efforts of Session and Presbytery to suppress it, continued, if not to thrive, at least to exist until after the Jacobite rising of 1715. In these days of religious toleration, when it is conceded that the Christian pilgrim may choose his church as freely as an ordinary traveller chooses his hotel, we would be moved to indignation by the treatment which the Episcopalians received from the Presbyterians in Kirkwall, but for the want of common sense evinced by the leaders of the persecuted party. Far from the centre of executive control, and patronised by the most influential of the local gentry, the rulers of the little Anglican synagogue became offensively aggressive.[59]

A Toleration Act of 1712 made Episcopal worship legal, but failed to win over Episcopalians in Orkney from their support for the Jacobite cause. Indeed, the Episcopalian clergyman and several of the lairds publicly proclaimed the Old Pretender as King at the Kirkwall Market Cross at Michaelmas, 1715, and drank the health of James VIII. In consequence, after the failure of the Jacobite Rising of '15, the London government took an interest in Orkney's potential traitors and required anyone wishing to travel south to obtain a certificate of loyalty from the Kirk Session or Presbytery. Non-Presbyterians were effectively placed under a form of 'house-arrest', confined to Orkney. Rev. James Lyon appears to have left Orkney in 1717 to escape prosecution. Hossack, writing in 1900, concluded:

> Thus, what persecution could not accomplish, self-interest did, and episcopacy in Kirkwall, having become inconvenient to its adherents, died a natural death. The story of the Meeting House troubles has recently been told with an episcopal bias, natural in the circumstances. No minister of the Established Church of Scotland would feel any pride in narrating the Presbyterian side of that story. Churches, like dogs, have their day, and, with true sectarian instinct, the stronger will try to worry the weaker. Dissent is now dominant in Kirkwall, and why should its history be devoid of the 'Meeting house' incident?

One glimmer of tolerance is seen in Hossack's telling of the story. Andrew Kerr, Presbyterian minister of the Second Charge at the Cathedral, was evidently a friend of James Lyon, the illegal Episcopal priest, on one occasion inviting him to his manse on the occasion of the baptism of his child. For this and other offences he was summoned to the Synod at Thurso (a regional church court between Presbytery and General Assembly) and was rebuked.

> [Mr Kerr] came a stranger to a town in a ferment of religious strife, when to belong to one party meant war to the knife with the other. To show friendship to an opponent was treason, and the only safety lay in consistent bitter partisanship.[60]

Outside of Kirkwall, the imposition of Presbyterianism by law had as great or greater an impact on the staffing of the parishes as the

Reformation had had. A Commission of General Assembly visited Orkney to examine the ministers as to their support for the new Establishment. Of a total of eighteen, only four conformed. Some were ejected, some were persuaded to resign; one was offered a pension. It seems that only the minister at Holm actually supported the new regime with any degree of enthusiasm. From the Holm Kirk Session Register:[61]

> Holm 30 May 1697. Qlk day ye min[iste]r did signifie to ye elderis yt now he was resolved to constitut and elect a new eldarship conform to ye order of the present Church government and inquyred if they were willing, who ansyrd they were.

Nevertheless, new ministers for the parishes came to replace the Episcopalian clergy. They faced a difficult situation for in general the lairds remained loyal to the Episcopal Church, in some cases employing episcopal priests as private chaplains.

Rev. John Brand, visiting Orkney in 1700 as part of the General Assembly's Commission, published a description of the county and its ministry at the opening of the eighteenth century. Provision of ministry had altered little since the end of the sixteenth century. The pattern of seventeen parishes and eighteen ministerial charges (Brand called them 'parishes') was given by him as follows:[62]

St Andrews and Deerness, including Copinsay	1 minister	2 kirks
Holm, including Lambholm	1 minister	1 kirk
Kirkwall and St Ola – a double charge	2 ministers	1 kirk (St Magnus)
Orphir	1 minister	1 kirk
Firth and Stenness, inc. Damsay	1 minister	2 kirks
Evie and Rendall inc. Gairsay	1 minister	2 kirks
Harray and Birsay	1 minister	2 kirks
Sandwick and Stromness inc. Careston	1 minister	2 kirks
with a note that Careston ought become separate, a parish to itself.		
Hoy and Graemsay	1 minister	2 kirks
Walls and Flotta	1 minister	2 kirks
South Ronaldsay and Burray	1 minister	3 kirks (2+1)
Shapinsay	1 minister	1 kirk

Stronsay and Eday and Faray	1 minister	2 kirks
with a note that Eday had a service every third Sabbath		
Sanday: Lady Kirk	1 minister	1 kirk
Sanday: Burness and Cross; and North Ronaldsay	1 minister	3 kirks (2+1)
Westray and Papay	1 minister	3 kirks (2+1)
Rousay with Eynhallow, Egilsay, Wyre	1 minister	2 kirks

Brand concluded:

> But there are 31 (sic) Kirks; And these Ministers look upon themselves as more happily posted, who have only one Kirk, especially if they have not more Kirks in several Isles, this tending more to the Edification of the People under their Charge, and consequently to their peace and encouragement, they every Lords-Day dispensing Ordinances in the same place, to the same People, whereas these who have more Kirks committed to them are sometimes obliged to preach in one place and sometimes in another, and the People generally frequent but their own Kirk, especially if they be in different Isles, hence ordinarily they enjoy the Ordinances only every other Sabbath, and in some places but one of three, which cannot but obstruct the progress of the Gospel, among them. Besides it is uneasy, expensive and dangerous for them to travel from Isle to Isle, and sometimes a storm arising they are necessarily detained there.

One hundred and forty years after the Reformation, the kirk in Orkney still could offer a regular, weekly, preaching ministry in only five of its seventeen charges. Elsewhere, the pattern was for the minister to alternate Sunday by Sunday with a single service in each of his buildings, and for the congregations to attend on a fortnightly basis. The provision of ministers, like the provision of schools, depended on the release of resources. Before the Reformation, Orkney's tithes had been largely allocated to the Cathedral. After the Reformation, those who held power in the land lacked interest in the Reformed Church – and after the Revolution of 1689, they were mainly Episcopalian. Besides, the Crown was the principal proprietor, and the government in London retained its own funds. The task of ministry for those who served the church was not easy. Brand wrote 'the stipends are small' and besides . . .[63]

> The ministers inform us, they were often in great danger in going to their

churches from Isle to Isle, visiting their Parishes, going to the Presbytery etc. Sometimes, pale death, with its graven countenance, presenting itself and staring them in the face, as one drawn out by the hairs of the head; another escaping on the keel of the overturned boat; sometimes they are arrested by a storm in the isles, and kept from their own families for some weeks.

Though Brand considered that 'the people are very tractable, submissive and respectful to their Ministers', his reports on the persistence of superstition might suggest that this 'submission' was mainly a matter of keeping away from trouble.

Bishop Robert Reid had concentrated resources at St Magnus. Bishop Adam Bothwell's lukewarm and financially compromised Reformation won few friends. Bishop James Law's principled Episcopacy helped to turn Orkney in a Jacobite direction, thus lessening the interest of the ruling class in the parish churches once Presbyterianism was restored. The uneducated section of the population remained superstitious and divided from the ministry by a considerable social gulf.[64] The Established Church at the beginning of the eighteenth century was hardly in a healthy spiritual position, although it enjoyed a monopoly of church life. The Reformation had sought an active, preaching ministry and a readily available educational system that would allow people to learn of Christ and follow Him with faith and understanding. Orkney, however, obtained the structure of a reformed church and its social discipline, without the heart of the faith seeming to catch alight. When spiritual revival did come, it was to challenge the Church by Law Established.

Towards the end of Hossack's *Kirkwall in the Orkneys* is a chapter on the 'Rule of the Church', written after careful examination of Kirk Session and Presbytery records. As with all such records of the period, they contain attempts to contain human morality by fallible legal processes, themselves tainted by social caste.[65] Hossack's comments are still worth reading, a century after they were written, though his commendation of the Catholic era is surely somewhat coloured by his own loyalties to Kirkwall itself and its Cathedral.[66] Nevertheless, Hossack takes us from the period of Bishop Robert Reid, through the Reformation and its sequel in denominational feuding and repression, towards the nineteenth century.[67]

> If, among her adherents, the Church of Rome allowed no diversity of opinion upon matters spiritual, and put down heresy with a high hand, in Orkney, where no heresy existed, her sway was mild and beneficent. Most of her prelates were men of wealth and influence, and they used these gifts for the adornment of their Cathedral, for the welfare of their people, and for the general improvement of their see.
>
> Following upon the Reformation came a series of churchmen, by turns Presbyterian and Episcopalian, as suited the politics of the day, but holding this, in common with the pre-Reformation clergy, that the priests were absolute rulers, and that passive obedience was the duty of the laity. In their hands the Decalogue became a code of civil law which gave them the power to interfere in the public business and the private affairs of every citizen . . . Kirkwall was well provided with ecclesiastical machinery for the reclaiming of backsliders. Outside the Cathedral were the Cuckstool, the Jougs, and the Stocks, while inside were the White Stone of Repentance, the Stool of Repentance, Sackcloth, the Prison, and the Minister – the last worst of all.
>
> It is ecclesiastical history and national experience that any country in the hands of an undivided church must be subject to priestly tyranny. This was the condition of Kirkwall down to the last decade of the eighteenth century, when, with dissent, came the dawn of freedom . . . Not that the Seceders were less strict than was the Church by law established . . . but, with a choice of churches, ministers were bound to be civil lest they should lose their customers.

After telling in brief the story of the various denominations established in Kirkwall in the nineteenth century, Hossack concludes:

> Without doubt there is a great waste of public money in the multiplication of churches and manses and stipends by denominations, the mass of whose adherents cannot tell the difference in doctrine or discipline which separate them from their neighbours. Yet the choice the layman has of sitting down under one of the many stocks of the Presbyterian vine, or enjoying the shade of Episcopal fig trees . . . banishes all fear of a renewal of the priestly tyranny to which our fathers were subjected before the days of dissent.

On Sunday 3 November 1996, as Moderator of the Presbytery of Orkney, I had the pleasure to be part of the Ordination service of the Revs. Inigrid Cosby and Eleanor Morson into the priesthood of the Episcopal Church of Scotland, by the Bishop of Aberdeen and Orkney. Bishop Bruce Cameron had invited Orkney clergy of other denominations to share in the service and in the laying on of hands at the point of ordination – and the service took place, not in the Episcopal Churches of either Stromness or Kirkwall, but in St Magnus Cathedral. Following the Ordination, the congregation took communion from one of three points, staffed by pairs of Presbyterian and Episcopalian clergy. As Moderator, I also welcomed Eleanor into corresponding membership of our Presbytery, for with consent of Presbytery, Kirk Session and the Kirk's appropriate national committee, she was appointed as Assistant part-time Minister at the Cathedral. Thus an Episcopalian priest took up office in the Cathedral to work with a Presbyterian minister and congregation: the rancour of the 'Meeting House controversy' had been totally forgotten!

Indeed, the working together and general good will between Christian denominations is one of the memorable features of Orkney church life. Stresses there still can be, particularly between the more and less charismatic; and hurt is still caused when individuals leave a congregation for another for personal or doctrinal reasons. There is a human tendency to allot blame: for the one leaving, to blame the failures that became intolerable; for the one left, to blame those who 'poached' a valued member. Nevertheless, especially on the islands, congregations include people originally brought up Catholic or Anglican or Methodist or whatever, now pleased to worship in the island kirk, whether or not they actually become members of the Presbyterian church. On Mainland, an ecumenical prayer group that many have found inspiring meets on Tuesdays in Kirkwall. Sunday services in the hospital and residential homes for the elderly are conducted in rota by the different denominations. I was myself invited to preach on different occasions by the Baptist, Congregational Church and Salvation Army congregations in Kirkwall.

Such was the spirit of co-operation that, in June 1995, Presbytery passed the following Declaration.

DECLARATION OF INTENT

We, members of the Presbytery of Orkney, recognise that, in a time of reappraisal such as this, we cannot effectively promote the mission and service of the Church in reliance upon the human and material resources which God supplies to any one part of the Church alone. We need to rely on the resources which God supplies to the whole Church of Jesus Christ.

We believe that, for the most effective co-operation of all Christian people, it is necessary to forego any positions of privilege or power, such as that of being the national Church, and to share the responsibilities which go with this, so that we may work on the basis of equality with all Christian people and better undertake the work of mission and service on these islands.

Until, therefore, the day comes when the Church of Scotland in General Assembly shares the responsibilities which are those of a national church and a new structure of ecumenical co-operation between denominations comes into being, we covenant to work equally with all our fellow Christians and their denominations on these islands for the promotion of the Kingdom of God.

'Working on a basis of equality with all Christian people' is a far cry from the turmoil and denominational strife that has marred the face of Kirkwall in previous centuries! Presbytery invited other denominations to open discussions on the possibility of covenanting to share in ministry together. By 1997, these were still ongoing, though most of the original participants withdrew, recognising that denominations still exist to represent genuinely-held doctrinal differences. Co-operation, rather than a formal covenant, seemed to many the best way forward. Perhaps B.H. Hossack, with his belief that difference guarantees freedom, would have approved.

His other comment, on the waste of maintaining multiple churches, manses and stipends, also sounds familiar after one hundred years. In all four charges for which I had responsibility in my four years in Orkney, the issue of which buildings to use loomed large. By the time I became its Interim Moderator, Sanday had demolished their Lady Kirk and were deciding whether to keep or sell the Cross Kirk too. North Ronaldsay, for its island population of less than ninety, had two church buildings, both in poor repair, but no money to fund the needed work.

After I handed over to Rev. Graeme Brown, Rousay decided to sell its church and, in partnership with the Orkney Islands Council (and with support from the Priority Areas Fund) developed its Manse as a Church Centre with a place of worship doubling with the community Triangle lunch club and day centre, and a flat for the visiting minister. Birsay's historic St Magnus Kirk was eventually given to a local Trust. Sandwick's St Mary's Kirk remained redundant, unwanted and unrepaired. On Hoy, the Presbytery attempted to close St John's, Lyness – and a General Assembly Commission nearly closed the damp St Columba's Kirk at Longhope instead. Throughout my time in the Presbytery, the Islands Council debated whether or not to buy the East Kirk in Kirkwall, a historic if crumbling building; meanwhile, the congregation there wished to move to and renovate their second building, the former King Street Free Church. All of these decisions about buildings caused controversy, sometimes anger, and certainly much time was diverted from essential Christian work.

Besides arguments about buildings, there were also discussions as to how many parishes and ministers the Church of Scotland ought to maintain; about how many stipends should be paid and/or could be afforded. Some annoyance was caused when the Presbytery Clerk, Rev. Trevor Hunt, in a discussion paper pointed out that, by following the national ratio of ministers to population, Orkney might qualify for one minister – never mind the fourteen we currently enjoyed! The ratio was certainly correct – but island situations are acknowledged to be different. How different, though? As always, finance was involved. Most small islands congregations, even linked parishes, cannot afford to pay a minister's stipend. Only the support of aid from the national church enables the north and south island ministries to continue. Wealthier parishes throughout Scotland are 'taxed' so that, after paying for their own needs, sums are available to be redistributed to communities and congregations 'on the edge'. It seems a pity that Orkney, through its elected representatives, seems so unaware of the investment and resources provided to its scattered communities by the Church.

In the context of our time, the principles of the Reformation and their outworking in Orkney still seem relevant. The pre-Reformation Catholic Church found that its traditional structure prevented effective communication of the Gospel; it even spoke a different language from the bulk of the population. It seems that today the language of educated theology is as remote as Latin from the experience of most; and the structures and constitution of the Kirk are equally as obscure. The energies and time of ministers are increasingly absorbed in Presbytery and national business, so recreating the pre-Reformation gulf between people and pastor. The liturgy and music of the Mass may well have been satisfying to those educated and trained to them, but as a mode of worship they had generally lost credibility; perhaps today the 'hymn-sandwich' is no longer plausible. The Reformed Church of 1560 sought a preaching ministry in order to revive spirituality and faith throughout the population in general, and never quite found the means to provide this in Orkney's scattered historic parishes. I hope that John Davidson's poetic strictures on the limits of what may be expected of one person may be remembered, together with his vision of reformed ministry. Linking larger with smaller islands, and also linking groups of Mainland parishes – even uniting them – has a long history behind it and a history not without its dangers. Yet the ultimate objective of the Reformation was not in fact centred on the ordained ministry: that was simply the tool for the job in the conditions of the time. In today's Orkney and today's Scotland, the task of reviving spirituality and faith throughout the population is surely to be attempted primarily by the ministry of the whole people of God.

---

1   When I was a boy at school, my final year history course specialised in the Reformation. At university, again the Reformation featured. After completing my training for the ministry, the opportunity arose of a three year research degree – I took as my topic the Scottish Reformation as it affected the counties of Angus and the Mearns. Coming to Orkney, I spent a little spare time researching the Reformation in Orkney. Eventually some notes became a talk at a Presbytery Christian Education Open Evening in October 1995, and then a talk to the Orkney Heritage Society in January 1996. These talks have been again expanded, and what follows is a tale of three bishops of Orkney – Robert Reid, Adam Bothwell and James Law – with a Presbyterian conclusion!
2   William P.L. Thomson, *A History of Orkney* (The Mercat Press, Edinburgh, 1987) p.125.
3   Gregor Lamb, *Testimony of the Orkneyingar – The Placenames of Orkney* (Orkney,

1993) p. 67.
4 Ernest W. Marwick, *The folklore of Orkney and Shetland* (B.T. Batsford Ltd, 1975) p. 14.
5 Ronald G. Cant, 'The constitution of St Magnus Cathedral' in ed. Barbara E. Crawford, *Northern Isles Connections* (The Orkney Press, 1995). See also Ian B. Cowan, 'The Organisation of Secular Cathedral Chapters' in ed. James Kirk, *The Medieval Church in Scotland* (Scottish Academic Press, 1995). Ian Cowan commented that the 1544 Constitution should not be taken at face value as, owing to the rights of existing holders of benefices, it did not come into effect immediately. A version of the text is given in ed. J.S. Clouston, *Records of the Earldom of Orkney 1299-1614* (Scottish History Society, 1914).
6 Ian B. Cowan, 'The Appropriation of Parish Churches' in ed. James Kirk, op.cit.
7 This table summarises the materials in Charles H. Haws, *Scottish Parish Clergy at the Reformation 1540-1574* (Scottish Record Society, 1972).
8 Ibid.
9 Raymond G. Lamb, *The Archaeological sites and monuments of Rousay, Egilsay and Wyre* (1982) p. 30 no. 146; Anna Ritchie, *Exploring Scotland's Heritage – Orkney* (1996) pp. 105-6; Rev. J.B. Craven, *History of the Church in Orkney 1558-1662* (Kirkwall, 1897) p. 72.
10 On 16 September 1550, the Crown offered a 19 year respite from prosecution to James Kaa, priest, chaplain in Orkney, accused for holding opinions contrary to Acts of Parliament; provided he abjured heresy and returned to Scotland: ed. D.H. Fleming & others, *Register of the Privy Seal of Scotland* (Edinburgh, 1921-1982), iv p. 916.
11 The Constitution is printed in *Records of the Earldom of Orkney*, pp. 363-71.
12 Well before 1560 it was generally agreed that Scotland's Church needed reforming. What was at issue was the pattern to be followed – that of the reformed Papacy, of the Council of Trent? Or the episcopal pattern of England? Or the more radical Protestantism of Calvin's Geneva? The last proved most suitable to the politics of the time – to a church whose reformation lacked royal enthusiasm.
13 trans./ed. Henderson and Bulloch, *The Scots Confession of 1560* (St Andrew Press, 1960); ed. James K. Cameron, *The First Book of Discipline* (St Andrew Press, 1972).
14 ed. T. Thomson, *Book of the Universall Kirk: Acts and Proceedings of the General Assembly of the Kirk of Scotland 1560-1618* (Bannatyne & Maitland Clubs, Edinburgh, 1839-45) i pp. 162-3. On Bishop Adam generally: Gordon Donaldson, 'Bishop Adam Bothwell and the Reformation in Orkney', *Records Scottish Church History Society* (1959) and, revised, in Gordon Donaldson, *Reformed by Bishops* (Edina Press, 1987). See also Rev. J.B. Craven, op.cit. (1897).
15 This and subsequent quotations from Mark Napier, *John Napier of Merchiston* (Edinburgh, 1834).
16 Peter D. Anderson, *Robert Stewart Earl of Orkney, Lord of Shetland 1533-1593* (John Donald, Edinburgh, 1982) p.32.

17 Arthur H. Williamson, *Scottish National Consciousness in the age of James VI* (John Donald, Edinburgh, 1979) p.14.
18 Peter D. Anderson, op.cit. (1982) p. 35.
19 Rev. J. Craven, *History of the Church in Orkney: From the introduction of Christianity to 1558* (Kirkwall, 1901) p.168.
20 Peter D. Anderson, op.cit. (1982) p.36. My translation of the quotation from Mark Napier, op.cit.: *gainstowd calland hymn and the laiff fullis that wist not quhatt thai did; and said he wald on na sort consent the mess wer donne.*
21 'Exhorter' was a temporary rank of subordinate preacher.
22 'Sixteenth Century Reform' in ed. Cant/Firth, op.cit. pp. 55-6.
23 Francis Bothwell and Thomas Beanston do not in fact appear on the national 'Register of Ministers, Exhorters and Readers', a document drawn up for November 1567.
24 'Register of Ministers, Exhorters and Readers' folio 73r to 75r. Scottish Record Office, E48.2.
25 Gordon Donaldson, *Reformed by Bishops* (1987) p. 28.
26 Rev. J. Craven, op.cit. (1897) p. 71.
27 Ibid, p. 20.
28 The opinions given here differ substantially from those of Gordon Donaldson, *Reformed by Bishops* (1987). Where there is no evidence that a priest served in the new church, I have assumed he did not. Professor Donaldson, however, very often assumed he did. It is crucial to understand that men continued to be known as Provost, Subchanter etc. and to enjoy the appropriate income, without that designation having any meaning for the reformed church.
29 Records Earldom of Orkney, p. 295.
30 Rev. J. Craven, op.cit. (1897) gives details of Foulsie and others of the reformed ministry from Charters seen by him.
31 Peter D. Anderson, op.cit. (1982) pp. 82-5.
32 Anna Ritchie, op.cit. (1996) p. 88. Painting Biblical scenes on the walls of churches was a practice that died after the Reformation – it continued a little longer in secular buildings.
33 Peter D. Anderson, *Black Patie: the life and times of Patrick Stewart, Earl of Orkney, Lord of Shetland* (John Donald, Edinburgh, 1992) p. 17.
34 Peter D. Anderson, op.cit. (1982) p. 92.
35 For the Stewart Readers, see the Tables of the reformed Ministry in Orkney 1560-1590 and also: John – Records Earldom of Orkney, p. 147, 354; Robert – Records Earldom of Orkney, p. 138, 289; Rev. J. Craven, op.cit. (1897) pp. 38, 40.
36 For the Henderson brothers, see the Tables of the reformed Ministry in Orkney 1560-1590 and also: Peter D. Anderson, op.cit. (1982) p. 176.
37 For further details see the Tables of the reformed Ministry in Orkney 1560-1590 and also: Peter D. Anderson, op.cit. (1982) p. 113 and appendix 6.
38 B.H. Hossack, *Kirkwall in the Orkneys* (Kirkwall 1900 and 1986) pp. 39-48.
39 'Trials for witchcraft, sorcery and superstition in Orkney' in *Miscellany of the Abbotsford Club* vol. i (Edinburgh, 1837).

40 For further details, see the Tables of the reformed Ministry in Orkney 1560-1590.
41 'Ane Dailog or Mutuall talking betuix a Clerk and ane Courteour concerning foure Parische Kirks till ane Minister', first published by Robert Lekprevick, St Andrews, 1574; now in ed. J. Cranstoun, *Satirical Poems of the Reformation* (Edinburgh and London, 1891). The line references to the quotations are, respectively: 475, 487, 504, 115, 483. See F.D. Bardgett, 'Four Parische Kirkis to Ane Preichir' in *RSCHS xxii*, 1986, p. 195f.
42 *MacFarlanes Geographical Collections vol. iii* (SHS 1908) pp. 302-24. Jo. Ben, whose names are probably both abbreviations and whose identity is disputed, claimed to have visited Orkney in 1527. Some of the events he mentioned happened after that year, however.
43 Peter D. Anderson, op.cit. (1992) p. 89.
44 Rev. John Brand, *A brief description of Orkney, Zetland, Pightland Firth and Caithness* (Edinburgh, 1701, reprinted 1883).
45 'The Craven Bequest' in the Scottish Record Office: SRO Gifts and Deposits 106.110.
46 William P.L. Thomson, op.cit. p. 238.
47 *Records Earldom of Orkney* pp. 254, 354; William P.L. Thomson, op.cit. pp. 238-9.
48 Moodie's career can be followed through the index of Peter D. Anderson, op.cit. (1982); also Rev. J. Craven, op.cit. (1897) pp.20-1; and SRO documents 'Register of Ministers and Readers', E48.2; 'Register of assignations and modifications of stipends' 1576-1615, E47.1. to E47.10. Printed editions of the former, and books based on these, wrongly suggest that Mr William Moodie was minister at South Ronaldsay and Burray before 1570.
49 Rev. J. Craven, op.cit. (1897) p. 49.
50 Peter D. Anderson, op.cit. (1992) pp.160, 55.
51 Ibid, (1992) pp. 49,50. Also Rev. J. Craven, op.cit. (1897) pp.66-70.
52 Peter D. Anderson, op.cit. (1992) – see index under 'Law'.
53 Rev. J. Craven, op.cit. (1897) generally and p.112.
54 Peter D. Anderson, op.cit. (1992) pp. 96-102, 117-33.
55 Alex. Peterkin, *Rentals of the Ancient Earldom and Bishopric of Orkney* (Edinburgh, 1620).
56 Hoy and Walls became separate parishes in 1632 – Rev. J. Craven, op.cit.(1897) p.167.
57 B.H. Hossack, op.cit. p. 248.
58 B.H. Hossack, op.cit. pp.284-5 suggests that the cost of the Covenanter Monuments, both in Deerness and on the Kirk Green, Kirkwall, was met by 'A visitor from South America' and not the outcome of 'Orcadian presbyterian enthusiasm' nor 'from Orcadian presbyterian pockets'. Nevertheless in 1888 when the Monuments were erected Kirkwall's church life was dominated by the United Presbyterian Church – one that viewed the Covenanters as among its spiritual ancestors. Rev. J. Craven's episcopalian sympathies are very obvious in his account of the 'Deerness Covenanters' – who, he suggests, had already seized the ship and were prevented

by the wreck from sacking St Magnus. Rev. J. Craven, *History of the Church in Orkney 1662-1688: The Restoration to the Revolution* (Kirkwall, 1893) pp.88-9.
59 B.H. Hossack, op.cit. pp.152, 238, 249.
60 Ibid p. 313. The story of the imposition of the Presbyterian establishment is also told from an episcopalian viewpoint in Rev. J. Craven, op.cit. (1893); and also Rev. J. Craven, *History of the Episcopal Church in Orkney 1688-1912* (Kirkwall, 1912).
61 Rev. J. Craven, op.cit. (1912).
62 Rev. John Brand, op.cit. pp. 42-62.
63 Rev. John Brand, op.cit. p.38.
64 William P.L. Thomson, 'The Eighteenth Century Church in Orkney' in ed. Cant/Firth, op.cit. (1989).
65 See also Paul J. Sutherland, 'Church Discipline and its Enforcement in Early Eighteenth Century Kirkwall' in *The Making of Modern Orkney – a selection of student essays* (University of Aberdeen, 1995).
66 The 1544 Charter spent the parishes' tithes and not Bishop Reid's personal wealth on St Magnus!
67 B.H. Hossack, op.cit. pp. 417, 443 and 459.

Tables of the reformed Ministry in Orkney 1560–1590

These tables are drawn up from the following sources:
- For 1562: ed. Gordon Donaldson, *Accounts of the Collectors of Thirds of Benefices* (SHS 1949). Other printed versions of the Accounts of the Collectors of Thirds are also to be found in the Orkney Room in Kirkwall.
- For 1567 and 1570: Scottish Record Office document E.48.2 – Register of Ministers and Readers, 1567–1572.
- For 1574: *Register of assignations and modifications of stipends* (Wodrow Society, 1844).
- For 1576 to 1590: Scottish Record Office documents E.47.1 to .10 – Register of assignations and modifications of stipends 1576 to 1615.

Abbreviations and key:
MINISTERS are shown in capitals:
Readers in lower case.

Mr = *Magister* = university Master's degree.
sir [lower case] = *dominus* = a Catholic priest, or one who was formerly a priest.

New entries are **distinguished** in **bold**.

Translations from parish to parish within Orkney are shown by arrows:

Parishes were unofficially linked until 1574 and this is shown by arrows:

At and after 1574 a national governmental reform rationalised linkages and stipends and the documents show a system of parishes served by a team of one minister and several readers.

During the 1580s policy emphasised the importance of a preaching ministry and the trend moved towards single-minister parishes where possible.

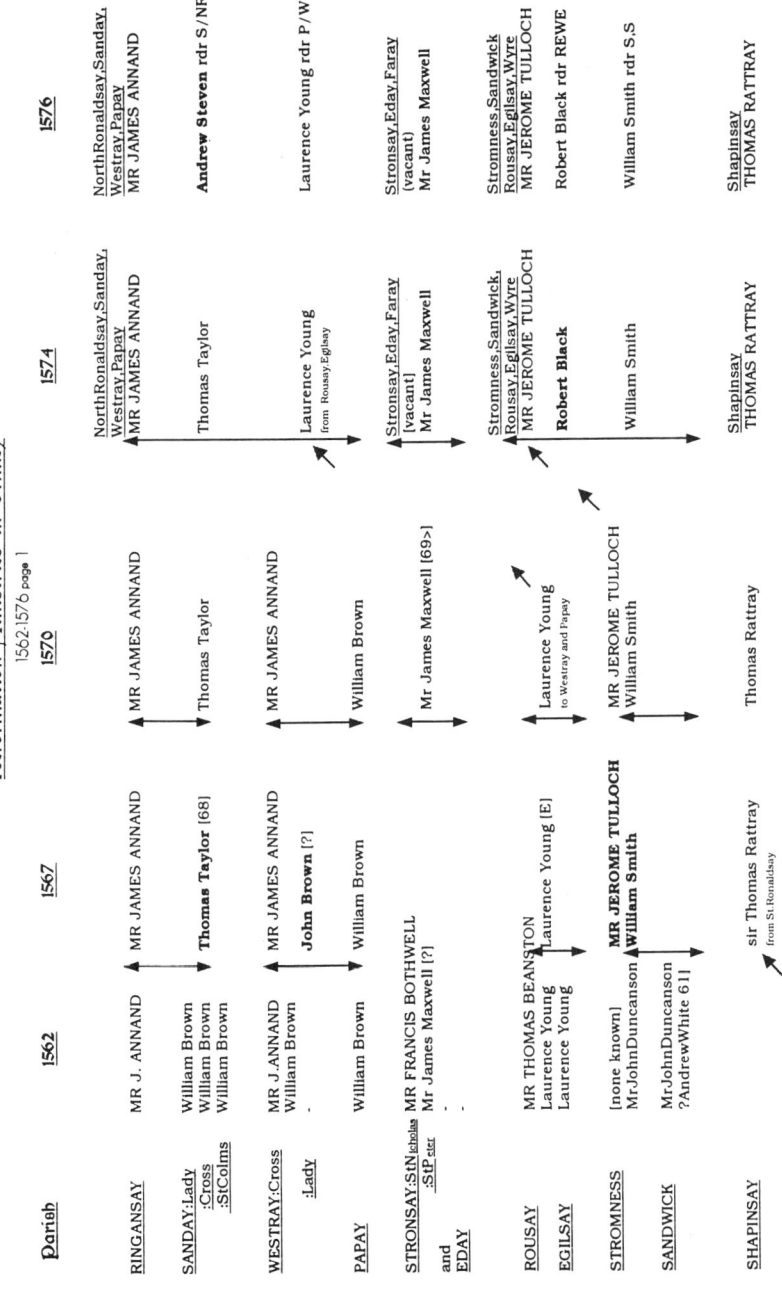

Reformation Ministries in Orkney
1562-1576 page 2

Parish	1562	1567	1570	1574	1576
EVIE	[none known>74] David Anderson	John Stewart to Holm/Deerness 70>	Archibald Reid >from StAndrews,Deerness	Orphir,Stenness, Evie,Firth,Rendall THOMAS STEVENSON	Orphir,Stenness, Evie,Firth,Rendall THOMAS STEVENSON
RENDALL	David Anderson			Archibald Reid	Archibald Reid rdr E.R
FIRTH	[none known]	THOMAS STEVENSON	THOMAS STEVENSON		
STENNESS and ORPHIR				William Muirhead	William Muirhead rdrS.F
BIRSAY and HARRAY	[none known]	MR DONALD WALKER Robert Stewart	?? Robert Stewart	Kirkwall, Birsay, Harray MR GILBERT FOULSIE Robert Stewart	Kirkwall, Birsay, Harray MR GILBERT FOULSIE Robert Stewart rdr B.H
KIRKWALL	MR G.FOULSIE	MR GILBERT FOULSIE John Sadler	MR GILBERT FOULSIE John Sadler	John Stewart and see Deerness, Holm below.	John Stewart rdr K
ST ANDREWS	[none known] Gavin Watt	MR DONALD BRUCE [?68] Gavin Watt Archibald Reid [68] to Evie,Rendall above >		StAndrews,Deerness Holm MR WILLIAM PEIRSON Mr John Houston rdr StA and Grammar School Schoolmaster	StAndrews,Deerness Holm MR WILLIAM PEIRSON Mr John Houston
DEERNESS	Gavin Watt	Gavin Watt Archibald Reid [68]			
HOLM	[none known] sir Nicol Craigie[E]	sir Nicol Craigie [E]	John Stewart from Evie/Rendall above	John Stewart rdr D.H and see Kirkwall above	John Stewart rdr D.H

96

Reformation Ministries in Orkney
1562-1576 page 3

Parish	1562	1567	1570	1574	1576
HOY	[none known]	John Mallson	**MR WILLIAM MOODIE** ←————→	Hoy,Walls,Graemsay, Flotta MR WILLIAM MOODIE	Hoy,Walls,Graemsay, Flotta MR WILLIAM MOODIE
WALLS	John Mallson				
FLOTTA	*	▶[Thomas Fleming?]	Thomas Fleming	Thomas Fleming	Thomas Fleming rdr
ST RONALDSAY	[none known] sir Thom.Rattray	**Duncan Ramsay**	←—— Duncan Ramsay [d.70]	St Ronaldsay, Burray, Swona **MR ALEXANDER DICK**	St Ronaldsay, Burray, Swona MR ALEXANDER DICK
BURRAY	sir Thom.Rattray to Sharpinsay	↗	▼ Edward Ingster [70>?]	←—— Edward Ingster	Edward Ingster
Diocese of Orkney					
Commissioner for Orkney		Mr James Annand [68>]	Mr James Annand	Mr James Annand	Mr James Annand
Commissioner for Shetland		Mr Gilbert Foulsie [68>]	Mr Gilbert Foulsie	Mr Gilbert Foulsie	Mr Gilbert Foulsie

Reformation Ministries in Orkney
1576-1590 page 1

[cf from 60-76]	1576	1580	1585	1588	1590
NorthRonaldsay,Sanday,		NorthRonaldsay,Sanday,	NorthRonaldsay,Sanday,	North Ronaldsay, Sanday MR ALEX CHEYNE [dltd 86] JAMES STEWART [dltd] MR JAMES COOK Andrew Steven	North Ronaldsay, Sanday MR JAMES COOK Andrew Steven
Westray,Papay	MR JAMES ANNAND Andrew Steven rdr S/NR Laurence Young rdr W/PW	Westray,Papay MR JAMES ANNAND Andrew Steven Laurence Young	MR ALEX CHEYNE Andrew Steven Westray, Papay MR ANDREW PITCAIRN Laurence Young	Westray, Papay MR ANDREW PITCAIRN Laurence Young	Westray, Papay MR ANDREW PITCAIRN Laurence Young
Stronsay,Eday,Faray	[vacant] Mr James Maxwell rdr	Stronsay,Eday,Faray WILLIAM HENDERSON Mr James Maxwell	Stronsay, Eday, Faray CUTHBERT HENDERSON Mr James Maxwell (StKatherine'sChap) rdr E,F '& no more readers to be admitted"	Stronsay, Eday, Faray CUTHBERT HENDERSON	Stronsay, Eday, Faray CUTHBERT HENDERSON
Stromness,Sandwick, Rousay,Eglsay,Wyre	MR JEROME TULLOCH Robert Black rdr REW Cuthbert Henderson REW [79] William Smith rdr S,S	Rousay,Eglsay,Wyre CUTHBERT HENDERSON Stromness, Sandwick MR JEROME TULLOCH William Smith	Rousay, Eglsay, Wyre MR NINIAN HALCRO ["Beanston provided of old and still living"] Stromness, Sandwick MR JEROME TULLOCH William Smith	Rousay, Eglsay, Wyre MR NINIAN HALCRO to StRonaldsay, below Stromness, Sandwick MR JEROME TULLOCH William Smith	Rousay, Eglsay, Wyre MR JAMES TULLOCH Stromness, Sandwick MR JEROME TULLOCH William Smith
Shapinsay	THOMAS RATTRAY	Shapinsay THOMAS RATTRAY	Shapinsay THOMAS RATTRAY	Shapinsay THOMAS RATTRAY	Shapinsay THOMAS RATTRAY
Orphir,Stenness, Evie,Firth,Rendall	THOMAS STEVENSON Archibald Reid rdr E,R William Muirhead rdrS,F	Evie,Rendall THOMAS STEVENSON Archibald Reid rdr E Robert Black rdr R Orphir, Stenness, Firth HARRY COLVILLE	Evie, Rendall, Eynhallow ROBERT BLACK Orphir, Stenness, Firth HARRY COLVILLE James Shorter	Evie, Rendall, Eynhallow ROBERT BLACK Orphir, Stenness, Firth HARRY COLVILLE James Shorter	Evie, Rendall, Eynhallow ROBERT BLACK Orphir, Stenness, Firth HARRY COLVILLE James Shorter
Kirkwall, Birsay, Harray	MR GILBERT FOULSIE Robert Stewart rdr B,H John Stewart rdr K [JS "son of the herald"]	Kirkwall, Birsay, Harray MR GILBERT FOULSIE Robert Stewart John Stewart	Birsay, Harray [vacant] Robert Stewart Kirkwall, St Ola THOMAS SWINTON John Stewart	Birsay, Harray [vacant] Robert Stewart Kirkwall, St Ola THOMAS SWINTON John Stewart	Birsay, Harray [vacant] Robert Stewart Kirkwall, St Ola THOMAS SWINTON John Stewart

Reformation Ministries in Orkney
1576-1590 page 2

[cf from 60-76]	1576	1580	1585	1588	1590
St Andrews, Deerness, Holm	MR WILLIAM PEIRSON Mr John Houston rdr StA John Stewart rdr D,H [JS "of Moray"]	StA/Deerness, Holm MR WILLIAM PEIRSON Mr John Houston John Stewart	StA/Deerness, Holm MR WILLIAM PEIRSON John Stewart	StA/Deerness, Holm MR WILLIAM PEIRSON John Stewart.	StA/Deerness, Holm MR WILLIAM PEIRSON
Hoy,Walls,Graemsay Flotta	MR WILLIAM MOODIE Thomas Fleming rdr	Hoy,Walls,Graemsay Flotta MR WILLIAM MOODIE Thomas Fleming	Walls, Flotta MR WILLIAM MOODIE Hoy, Graemsay, THOMAS FLEMING	Walls, Flotta MR WILLIAM MOODIE Hoy, Graemsay, THOMAS FLEMING	Walls, Flotta MR WILLIAM MOODIE Hoy, Graemsay, THOMAS FLEMING
St Ronaldsay Burray, Swona	MR ALEXANDER DICK Edward Ingster rdr	St Ronaldsay, Burray, MR ALEXANDER DICK Edward Ingster	St Ronaldsay, Burray, ALEX CALLENDER Edward Ingster	St Ronaldsay, Burray, ALEX CALLENDER Edward Ingster	St Ronaldsay, Burray, MR NINIAN HALCRO Edward Ingster
Diocese of Orkney Commissioner for Orkney:	Mr James Annand	Mr James Annand			
Commissioner for Shetland	Mr Gilbert Foulsie	Mr Gilbert Foulsie			
Commissioner for Orkney and Shetland			Thomas Swinton	Thomas Swinton	Thomas Swinton

Chapter 5

Secession, Disruption and Reunion, 1790–1929

The Legacy of the Secession in Kirkwall

The eighteenth century saw a reaction to the spiritual enthusiasm that fed the civil wars in Scotland and England. Scottish Church leaders urged 'moderation': a rational faith and decorous behaviour.[1] Socially close to the lairds who were their patrons, the ministers of the Established Church were distanced from their congregations. In consequence, as waves of revival swept Scotland during the century, an increasing number of congregations and ministers left the Established Church and formed their own Presbyterian denominations, free from the connection with the state. These Secession Churches aimed to maintain what they believed were the achievements of the Reformation and subsequent Covenanting times: a church whose theology was based on the Calvinism of the Westminster Confession, whose congregations were free to call their own ministers, which sought purity both of belief and personal conduct. Intense personal spirituality, learnt from rigorous preaching of the Bible, drove the leaders of Secession congregations.

The origins of the Secession congregations in Orkney, therefore, lay in dissatisfaction with the existing establishment. In 1796, a new Kirkwall congregation tapped into such a dissatisfaction with the provision of public worship and ministry based on St Magnus Cathedral that in just a few years, an independent church a thousand strong sprang into existence. Several elements of dissatisfaction can be identified, though in the records and biographies written to tell the story of the Secession Church, the key reason for leaving the Church of Scotland was its failure to proclaim the gospel. Listen to the third Secession minister, David Webster, writing in 1896:

There is evidence enough that the Established Church was then in a very deplorable condition. Evangelical preaching was almost, if not altogether, unknown; and indeed there was little preaching of any kind – not even of the cold moderate type that was practised elsewhere. The ministers were proverbially indolent and inefficient, remiss in their duties, and some of them not over decent in their lives. The inhabitants being scattered over 14 or 15 islands separated by open and dangerous firths, and two and sometimes three parishes being placed under the charge of one minister, it was no uncommon thing that for months together some of the islands were left without any Sabbath service [and then that] being for the most part destitute of saving gospel truth.

At issue, of course, was what was meant by 'The Gospel'. The 'Moderate' ministers of the Established Kirk before 1800 reflected the theology of their day, a theology that had moved away from the traditional Calvinism of Scotland. The second Secession minister, Dr Paterson, writing in 1824, accused the Kirk not of *not* preaching, but of preaching the *wrong* gospel. Writing against a defender of the Orkney clergy, he asked:

Does he know of [one] who, in a discourse, openly impugned the doctrine of election, and characterised it as a tenet held by weak minds? Does he know [of one who] attacked some of these same doctrines of grace with such unhallowed fury, as to declare that they represented God 'instead of a merciful Friend, as a merciless fiend'? Does he know of [another] who gave a direct public denial to the doctrine of justification by grace, and avowedly taught that man might and could be justified by works?

This was an era dominated by the Westminster Confession of Faith, the key doctrinal statement of the Presbyterian churches. Agreed by English and Scottish Churches during the period of the Civil War, the Confession embodies the doctrinal scheme of developed Calvinism, summarised by some of its proponents as 'double predestination'. According to this school of thought, the Lord God had, before the creation of the world, assigned or predestined all of humanity, some to heaven and some to hell: a judgment that no choice made by man, woman or child could alter. The 'moderate' ministers of Orkney's Established Kirk appear to have rejected this traditional scheme of doctrine, considering that such a doctrine of election 'represented God, instead of a merciful Friend, as a merciless fiend'. Followers of the Secession Fathers, however, rejected modernist thinking and held to the traditional theology of Scotland as 'the pure gospel'.

Besides these high matters of theology, other more mundane matters probably played a part in the popularity of the Secession Church in Kirkwall. It is said that craftsmen involved in the Secession had their own conflicts with the Kirk Session of St Magnus over what fees were payable for funerals. Moreover, St Magnus itself was thought most unsuitable for comfortable worship. Early in the nineteenth century, the more evangelical section of its membership petitioned that a new Church of Scotland should be built in Kirkwall.

> Petition to the Presbytery of Kirkwall,
> That there is no proper Parish Church for accommodating the inhabitants either of the Burgh of Kirkwall or of the landward district of St Ola – the ancient Cathedral of the bishops of Orkney having been used for that purpose since the Revolution. That fabric however is so old and damp, that it is unsafe for the petitioners and others to attend public worship in it (particularly during the winter season) and the space fitted up as a place of worship is so limited that it is totally insufficient to hold even a small proportion of the population, entitled by law to be accommodated with seats in their parish church . . . The Dissenting meeting house, containing 1200, is insufficient for the wants of those who attend it, many of whom frequent it because they cannot get accommodation at all or without endangering the safety of their health attend in the established church of which they are members.

A second Established congregation was in fact created, and a building built for it, known as 'The East Kirk'; this building no longer survives.

Finally, and I think I am right to place this last in the case of Orkney, came the principle on which the Secession Fathers first split from the Church of Scotland back in 1733. Their first minister, Ebenezer Erskine, rejected the right of Parliament and the state Courts to enforce the privilege of landlords (known as *heritors*) to nominate the ministers of the Established Church. The Secession went on to claim the right of the Church in Scotland to be free of state control. Secession Churches, in fact, thought of themselves as the true Church of Scotland, preaching the Reformation gospel of God's grace, claiming the freedom for the Church enjoyed by Knox's generation. Before 1560, when protestant congregations were illegal, the reformed lairds and burghs had chosen and protected their own preachers. After 1560, in theory congregations were given the right to elect their ministers. In practice, those who had the legal right to present clients to the benefice usually controlled appointments. During the first decades of the eighteenth century, Parliament in London confirmed the rights of patrons to nominate parish clergy in Scotland – and so provoked the first Secession of 1733. A second followed in 1761. In many respects the various branches of the Secession denominations shared the inheritance of the Established Church and they followed the same patterns of worship – but they claimed the right of freedom from governmental control, from the control of the Westminster and Edinburgh establishments. Separate they might be, but the Secession were still Scottish Presbyterians.[2]

A prayer meeting had begun in Kirkwall in 1790 whose members sought a 'gospel ministry' in the town similar to that some of them had known when working south. They obtained land for a church in 1793,

The 'Paterson Kirk', Kirkwall

and a building to seat eight hundred opened in 1796; a Kirk Session was elected that year and congregational life began with a variety of visiting preachers to supply the pulpit. The first minister, Mr William Broadfoot, from Whithorn, was called and began in 1797 a ministry to a congregation estimated at over five hundred. Such was the success of the new church that its building was demolished and rebuilt to seat 1200 in 1798.

The Secession Congregation was evangelical, believing in its duty under God to win people for Christ at home and abroad. Their letters and papers of the time speak of the need for 'an aggressive spirit' of religion. Financially supported only by their own generosity, new congregations followed the example of the Kirkwall church. At first, enthusiasts from all over Orkney occasionally attended worship in Kirkwall. Once a local nucleus had been identified, they also began worship in their own community in temporary accommodation with visiting preachers. Funds were raised to acquire a site and build a church. Finally, sufficient promises of regular giving having been made to support a minister, the congregation's independent existence was recognised. The following table charts the creation of Secession congregations in Orkney.

During Mr William Broadfoot's ministry (1797–1817):
Sanday 1800
Stronsay 1800
Birsay 1801
Stromness 1803
Holm 1814

During the ministry of Dr Robert Paterson (1820–1870):
Westray 1821
South Ronaldsay 1826
Eday 1828
Rousay 1829
Sandwick 1829
Shapinsay 1831
Firth 1835
Burray 1855

During the ministry of Mr David Webster (1865 as colleague; 1870–1903):
>	Egilsay 1883 as a Mission of Kirkwall
>	Rendall 1885: congregation previously independent and opted to become a UP Mission of Kirkwall.

In the rural parishes as with Kirkwall, it is possible in retrospect to see other factors apart from the purely spiritual that may have contributed to the success of the Secession. In his book *Auld Peedie Kirks*, W.M. Gibson traces the history of the church in Stronsay, and reprints documents from around 1800 showing conflict between the larger farmers and the smaller tenants and crofters. The nation-wide push towards 'improvement' in agricultural practice too often meant the over-riding of crofting or udal traditions. The well-to-do tried to block peat-cutting rights, and to prevent communal pasturing by enclosing fields. Ministers of the Established Church, who owed their livings to the patrons and obtained their stipends from the tithes paid by these larger farmers, must have seemed often unsympathetic to the claims of the majority. Given a choice, many of the less well off preferred to choose their spiritual support from elsewhere – from the Secession.[3]

Being thus composed of independently minded people of limited resources did not make for an easy life for several of the rural congregations. William Taylor, second Secession minister in Stronsay, was driven to demit in 1823 when an influential section of his congregation objected to his marriage to the daughter of a farmer engaged in improvement in the island. With promised donations to his stipend withheld and members withdrawing from worship and meeting privately for prayer, Mr Taylor had little choice – even though he had the support of the other ministers. The divisions caused were still evident in the 1870s and played a part in the demission of the fourth minister, David Buchanan. Meanwhile, the Birsay congregation had ceased its connection with the mainstream Secession denomination when Synod attempted to discipline their minister, Archibald Willison, in 1807. Troubles between John Pettigrew and a section of the Holm congregation resulted in a faction breaking off to join the Free Church in 1869. The official *History of the U.P. Congregations* also provides evidence of the difficulty some Orkney congregations had in raising sufficient funds to pay their ministers. Sanday, for example, did not become self-supporting until 1868.[4]

The Kirkwall congregation itself suffered a secession in 1805 when a number of members left to help create an Independent Church that became the town's Congregational Church. Nevertheless, when the *UP Record* for 1896 chronicled the congregation's celebration of its first one hundred years, it rightly took a congratulatory tone. Looking back after a further hundred years and trying to recall the history and principles of our predecessors, it is worth examining this account to see what they said about themselves. The Rev. David Webster wrote in the *UP Record,* Oct. 1894:

> It is something to be said of a congregation that for a 100 years it has had a pure gospel uninterrupted and faithfully preached from its pulpit and a succession of elders . . . who, perhaps with one or two exceptions, have been worthy and exemplary men, diligent in the discharge of their official duties. This and more than this can be said of the congregation here. It has done much to promote the social, educational and religious welfare of the Orkney people, and has been also distinguished for its liberality in the cause of foreign missions. By its agencies it has instructed and trained a vast number of young people in the Christian faith . . .

Taking these elements identified for us, the principles that were dear to the Dissenters of Kirkwall were as follows:

First, 'a pure gospel preached'. Secession churches were from the beginning missionary churches – evangelical churches – churches that appealed to households and individuals to come to repentance, to deeper commitment, to personal faith. But these are terms that, though familiar, do in fact differ in their use from generation to generation. It is best to allow Dr Paterson and Mr Webster to speak for themselves. So, from Dr Paterson in 1860:

> I have to think of my mission to this place, I am here to fulfil the ministry of reconciliation – to deal in Christ's name with my fellow-men regarding the awful matters of their relations with God, and their interests for eternity – to declare to them the truth on such subjects as their apostasy, their ruined nature, their imperilled interests, the provision of Divine

love for their deliverance, the glorious amplitude of that provision, the offer of its priceless blessings to them, and the issues that are at stake. Especially, I may say with emphasis, I am here to proclaim the one great Saviour – to declare who and what the Saviour of the world is – to speak of the wonders of the God-man and His work – to exhibit Him in His death and His life, His cross and His crown, as the wisdom of God unto salvation, as able to save to the uttermost all who come to God by Him – I am here to hold up the glorious Saviour to the view of men, clearly, closely, and consistently, that they may look to Him and live, believe in Him and be saved – to tell them what they may have in Him, – that they may have reconciliation with God by His blood, a renovated nature by His Spirit, and eternal life as His gift . . . And so it is that I am here to watch for souls – to seek the conversion of sinners and the holiness of Christians . . .

What did the minister mean by 'as able to save to the uttermost all who come to God by Him'? How did such a wide offer of salvation – 'all' – relate to the doctrine of predestination? There were some evangelicals in the Secession Church in the south who believed that an open offer of salvation to all – to all the world – was incompatible with the Westminster Confession, and so left to begin a new denomination: the Morrisonians, or Evangelical Union. Missionaries from this group visited Kirkwall in 1841, but had no success. Dr Paterson held sway, persuading his flock that they could hold to the doctrine of the Confession *and* proclaim Christ 'as able to save to the uttermost all who come to God by Him'.

The 'pure gospel', then, was an open gospel, a gospel for all, a gospel of Christ, preached in traditional Biblical terms. During the late 1830s, Dr Paterson led his people towards Revival. Following the American preacher Charles Finney, Dr Paterson believed that if ministers 'make sure use of the divinely appointed means of a revival, and if they put these into operation, and work them vigorously, much will be done.' He devised his own 'course of revival preaching', and held Session meetings to 'attend to the subject of revival'. He viewed his ministry as the centre of a 'holy, aggressive agency, having a wide circumference' besides his own flock to 'places scantily supplied with the bread of life, unbefriended islands – souls uncared for.'

This, too, was the gospel preached by David Webster: 'the full, free and unqualified offer of the Gospel to all sinners without exception.' David Webster wrote in the *Record* for July 1894:

> The love of God embraces us all; the invitations of the gospel have respect to us all; the blessings it offers are amply abundant to enrich us all; and in the home of the redeemed there is room for us all. If any of us never reach that home it will not be because it was barred against us; it will not be because we were not invited to enter; it will not be because our loving God was unwilling to receive us; it will not be because the gracious Saviour had not His compassionate eye upon us when He died to save; it will not be because the Holy Spirit did not strive with us; it will only be because that, notwithstanding all that has been done for us – all the mercy and love and long suffering of God, who is not willing that any should perish – we rushed on to our own destruction. We have said that the love of God and the invitations of the gospel have respect to us all; and of this the Word of God gives us ample assurance.

With such an emphasis on the text 'not willing that any should perish' [2 Peter 3:9] some distancing has occurred from the double predestination of the early Secession – from the scornful dismissal of the Established Kirk moderates who could not accept such a doctrine of election. Nevertheless, it was important to both Dr Paterson and Mr Webster that they preached 'the pure gospel'.

In 1843 a further national evangelical denomination broke from the Established Church, seeking to alter the constitutional relationship between the state and the kirk – the Free Church of Scotland, which founded its own congregations in Orkney. The Free Kirk, in principle and like the Church of Scotland, believed that the state should establish and sponsor the church – but they objected to its interference in spiritual matters. The Secession Churches, however, were 'voluntaries'; they believed that Christian people should support the church by voluntary work and giving, and opposed the privileges conferred by 'establishment'. By 1891, three major Presbyterian denominations maintained congregations in many of Orkney's parishes: The Church of Scotland, The Free Church and the United Presbyterian Church. Of these, it is reckoned that the UPs had the largest membership – Orkney was the only county in Scotland where this was so.[5] In the course of less than a hundred years, the Secession had won the support of a majority of those Orcadians who thought of themselves as Presbyterian. Not that all of Orkney by the nineteenth century was Presbyterian. William Tulloch (from North Ronaldsay), under the inspiration of the roving Scottish evangelist James Haldane, founded in Westray in 1803 what was to become Orkney's first Baptist Church, restricting membership to those who had accepted adult or believers' baptism. Other Baptist congregations or preaching stations came into being on Eday, Burray (which supported meetings on Flotta and South Ronaldsay) and Sanday.[6] From the early Baptist congregations also sprang the Brethren Fellowships, who rejected the necessity for a separate or ordained ministry, and created a network of Gospel Halls. Kirkwall, meantime, though it had no Baptist Church until the twentieth century, was home to an Independent or Congregational Church, and (from 1871) to a congregation of the Scottish Episcopal Church. When *Kirkwall in the Orkneys* was written, B.H. Hossack noted that the Salvation Army had 'recently invaded Kirkwall'. He also recounts that 1877 saw the consolidation of an earlier Catholic mission by the building of a Church in Kirkwall.[7]

Besides their evangelical character, Orkney's Secession churches were distinguished by:
- a concern for education – running their own Sunday Schools and programmes of adult learning;
- a concern for the poor – giving to their own scheme for relief;
- a concern for personal morality, supporting the Temperance Movement;
- a Missionary emphasis: collecting funds and holding prayer meetings for mission at home and in the Empire;
- progressive worship in modern buildings, based on Biblical preaching and including a strong musical input;
- support for progressive movements in society: politically Liberal, encouraging state education and opposed to privilege.

Returning to the text: *for a 100 years [this congregation] has had a pure gospel uninterrupted and faithfully preached from its pulpit and a succession of elders . . . who, perhaps with one or two exceptions, have been worthy and exemplary men, diligent in the discharge of their official duties.* A succession of elders, *diligent in their official duties.* What were the duties of the eldership in the Secession? Dr Paterson provided guidelines for his elders in 1828, and had them recorded in the Session Minutebook.

> *Charge to Elders, containing hints which may be useful to guide them in the pastoral visitations of the members of their districts.*
>
> *Public Worship* – See that they are regular in their attendance forenoon and afternoon. If circumstances do not allow all the members of the family to attend regularly, take heed lest any one member should make that a cloak for being habitually or frequently absent. Where there is regularity in attendance, take heed that other visible sinful and improper habits be not contracted – such as coming late to church; sleeping in it; obviously inattentive hearing; worldly conversation on the way to or from it.
>
> *Fellowship meetings* – Encourage them; excite members to join them; endeavour to prevent members from withdrawing from them.
>
> *Family worship* – Treat the subject cautiously. Endeavour by prudent means to ascertain whether it is regularly maintained or not. If it be not, try to come to some right understanding about the cause – whether it be the mere force of previous habits, or any particular decline in religion, or domestic disorder.
>
> *Self-government* – Watch carefully over the temperance of your members; give no toleration to any habit of tippling. Decidedly discountenance the unwarrantable habit of going into public-houses. . . . Reprove and try to repress all sallies of angry and sinful passions, and excite to the cultivation and display of a meek and Christian temper.
>
> *Duties to Children* – See that their education – and especially their spiritual instruction – be not neglected . . .
>
> *The Sick* – Manifest your Christian sympathy with them; visit them; counsel them; console them; pray with them.
>
> *The Poor* – Be well acquainted with them. Attend to their interests; see that no case of actual want be unattended to. But, even at the risk of giving offence, repress all symptoms of greed, murmuring, quarrelling with the Session or with the supplies of others. Beware of encouraging habits of dependence, or mean and beggarly dispositions.
>
> *Other relative duties* – take heed that your members be not deceitful or over-reaching in their dealings, but men of uprightness; see that they do not trifle with their obligations to pay their lawful debts. Be concerned to check calumnious or evil speaking, the retailing of idle and injurious reports, and the varied symptoms of bitterness of feeling towards fellow-

members and others; as far as possible, check idle and unwarrantable prying into the domestic concerns of others.

The *Record* provides obituaries for some of these men (for men they were and not women): stalwarts of the congregation from the early days, coming at last to be buried during David Webster's ministry.

Mr John White [*UP Record* January 1885]
His connection with the congregation dates from 1818. He was at that time a young man of earnest piety. During the summer months he and five or six like-minded companions were in the habit of rising early on Sabbath mornings and proceeding together to a cave in the rocks facing the sea at Berstane, where they spent an hour in devotional exercises; and again, when the public services of the day were over, they met for prayer in one or other of the houses in which they lodged. In 1822 he began to teach in the Sabbath-School, and continued faithfully at the work for about fifty years, when growing infirmity compelled him to retire. He was elected to the Eldership in 1835 . . . Mr White possessed in a marked degree the essential qualifications for the office he so long and creditably filled. His piety was genuine; he was well acquainted with the great doctrines of scripture; and he was thoroughly evangelical in sentiment and feeling.

Mr William Laughton [*UP Record* January 86]
He was a man of general intelligence, not so much from the extent and variety of his reading, for it was confined very much to literature of the kind which bears upon the higher life and the interests of eternity. But he was shrewd and observant and thoughtful, and could gather information from sources which would not have yielded it to less discerning men. In all the details of business he was strictly truthful and upright, and to his engagements sacredly punctual. He was 'mighty in the scriptures', and strongly attached to the system of doctrine summarised in the Shorter Catechism. As an elder he was faithful to his duties . . .

Mr James Robertson [*UP Record* July 89]
He was naturally quiet, amiable and unobtrusive. When elected to the eldership, he shrank from its responsibilities, but when called upon to give his answer, he did not see his way clear to refuse the call of the church to office. None was more regularly in Church on Sabbath than

he, and none was more constant in attendance at the quarterly meetings of Session. He was not a leader in church affairs – he had not the qualifications for that – but his interest in all that concerned the church was genuine. The usefulness of an elder can be measured pretty exactly as a rule by his helpfulness to the minister in his work. No one could have been more helpful, in ways in which a minister perhaps most of all feels his need of help. By his love, by his kindliness, by his sympathy, by his prayers, he was helpful. Give a minister these, and you contribute much to the success of his ministry. The loss of an elder like James Robertson is no small loss to the congregation . . .

The UP Congregation came to include many of those who led society in Kirkwall. Though he was not an elder, the death of Mr James Cumming, of the store Cumming and Spence, was recorded in April 1897. Mr Webster commented it had been pleasing to see Mr Cumming in church Sunday by Sunday for both services: 'an intelligent worshipper, and a prayerful and attentive hearer of the Word.' James Cumming's final will left bequests to the Balfour Hospital, the Orkney Branch of the National Bible Society, the Magistrates of Kirkwall to provide coal for the poor in winter, £500 to support the ministry of his church and £1000 for the Foreign Missions of the UP Church. With such leaders, it is no wonder that the congregation could claim to have

Rev. David Webster, minister of the United Presbyterian congregation, Kirkwall [from a 19th century photograph]

achieved much in the fields of the *social, educational and religious welfare* of Kirkwall.

Temperance was a major UP interest; Mr Webster was instrumental in the creation of Temperance Associations, both Adult and Juvenile, in 1885 – though total abstention was never a requirement for members. During the closing years of Mr Webster's ministry, in 1888, he denounced from the pulpit a drunken breach of the Sabbath by some four or five hundred sailors and marines from the Channel Fleet, who caroused throughout the day throughout the burgh.

> In the course of the day 400 or 500 seamen and marines came ashore, and as the evening advanced, our streets became a scene of the most revolting revelry and drunkenness. I am within the truth when I say that dozens of men in uniform of the ships might have been seen, one here and another there, lying in a state of helpless intoxication. The ears of the sober passer-by were shocked with the sounds of ribaldry and profanity that everywhere assailed them. Bacchanalian songs were sung and chorused to the echo, till the noise of the revelry was heard afar. Never within the memory of the oldest inhabitant was such a desecration of the Sabbath seen in Kirkwall. It was humiliating and shameful in the extreme.

Mr Webster asked 'Who was to blame?' and found answers in the Fleet's officers, the Hotel and Public House owners who had opened their doors, those who provided boats to ferry the men ashore, and the Magistrates of the Burgh. He called upon all in sympathy with the Temperance Associations and the preservation of the Sabbath to exercise their vote accordingly at the next Council elections.

Such a call might well have been heeded. Five years before, Mr Webster had been influential in the welcome extended by Orkney to the then Liberal Prime Minister, Gladstone, who was given the Freedom of the Burgh at a public ceremony within the UP Church – the East Kirk. It says much about the high standing of the UP congregation in Kirkwall's civic affairs that such a public occasion should be held in 'The Paterson Kirk'.

It should be emphasised that the Secession congregations, though conservative in theology, could be socially forward-looking. They thought of themselves as progressive; they said that 'Christianity is a religion of progress'. They were engaged in the restructuring of Scottish society; they worked for the abolition of the rights of lairds over the parish churches, the abolition of the right of the established church to control education, the ending of the tithe as a compulsory tax to support an established church. Dr Paterson's political sympathies were given to the Liberal cause. In the *Memoirs* of him written by his brother, we learn that he supported publicly the Great Parliamentary Reform Act of 1832, the abolition of slavery in the Empire and the disestablishment of the Irish Church. In the latter cause, dear to Dissenting hearts, he took an active part in the Parliamentary elections of 1868.

> I was obliged to go to the electoral hustings yesterday, by which, I daresay, my cold was increased. The county contest is desperately keen. Tory landlords are doing their best and their worst to oust Dundas. Their new man thinks us sad thorns in his flesh. I had thought I might escape any political immersion at this time, but no. This Irish Church question carries so much in it, that one must think, speak and act. The pressure on me at present is great.

As early as 1830, the Secession minister had been the toast of the political worthies who gathered at pre-election fund-raising dinners. Dr Paterson, writing to his brother:

> We have had a time of great bustle in the town. I was at both the election dinners. At that for the county I had the honour of having my health drunk. The half of the money which the Member, Mr Traill of Hobbister, left for the poor, was placed at my disposal. I never saw the tide of feeling in favour of the Secession, among the upper ranks, so strong.

At his death, it was recorded of Dr Robert Paterson, that *'his political and social influence was very advantageous to the Liberal Cause in Orkney. He was often in correspondence with persons of position and authority, regarding questions which involved the public welfare, so that the* Scotsman *newspaper, remarked, "He possessed an influence in the county greater far than any other man".'*

Believing in the popular election of both ministers and elders, both

Dr Paterson and David Webster went with the tide of growing democracy in the nineteenth century. As British influence expanded round the globe, so did the missionary work of the UP Church. This was a Church conscious of going with the tide of events – the tide of progress. Dr Paterson in 1839:

> Christianity has many essential characteristics, and among these progress is one. It is essentially a religion of progress.[8]

In 1895, David Webster used the same logic when members of the congregation opposed the decision to add central heating and ventilation to the church building as part of their celebration of their centenary.

> Consider what improvements have been introduced into our whole social system since the church we now worship in was built. Our dwelling-houses are better; our public buildings, our places of business, our warehouses and workshops, our schools and colleges, and even our prisons, are all vastly improved. We live in an age of progress, and is there to be progress in all conditions of social and domestic life and no progress in matters that show a very direct bearing on the interests of religion? We can suppose that when the present church was projected there were some who looked askance at the movement on the plea that what had served the past generations was good enough for the generations to come. But it is perfectly certain that if these objectors had had their own way no one would have benefited from their penurious policy, and the good cause which our church in Orkney has so long and worthily represented would have lost immensely. We would not have held the influential position in the community which we hold today, and the missionary and benevolent work which, by the blessing of God, we have been enabled to do during the last half century would not have been accomplished. And so there may possibly be some in the congregation now who think that the church as it is, having served the past generation, is all that is required for the future . . . But that is a style of reasoning that cannot bear to be looked at. It is unjust to ourselves, it is ungenerous to our children, and it is prejudicial to the cause of Christ.

The leadership of the UP Church in 1895, planning for their centenary celebrations, decisively rejected the view that their first duty was to preserve unaltered the legacy of the past. Progress – as an essential characteristic of the Christian faith – a sense of moving on, of attempting new things, of reshaping the world by the Gospel and the voluntary and sacrificial effort of Christian people; this sense of progress was at the heart of the leadership of the Paterson Kirk. The Kirkwall: East congregation is in fact the successor to both the UP Paterson Kirk and the Kirkwall Free Kirk: these two congregations between them built seven church buildings and two halls in the nineteenth century. They built and demolished buildings to suit what they needed – to serve the interests of religion – the progress of the cause of Christ.

Progress in the area of the education of children was a field dear to the hearts of the Secession. In this they were in the tradition of the Scottish Reformation, whose first leaders had a vision of a school in every parish. By the early nineteenth century, the main provision of schools was those parish schools controlled by the Established Kirk Session, who selected and employed the Dominie, and set the level of fees to pay his stipend. This was a system bitterly criticised by the Secession.

> You ask my opinion on the educational question. It is one surrounded with difficulties; but I have no difficulty in indicating our present line of duty. It is towards the overthrow of the present parochial system. Whatever system may be right, that system is wrong, – wrong in its presbyterian management, wrong in its sectarian exclusiveness, wrong in its life appointments. The parochial schools of Orkney are in a state of the most lamentable inefficiency. The average attendance at several of them during the year did not exceed eight or ten pupils, while the education obtained at many of them is of the meanest and most trifling kind. We should direct ourselves to the overthrow of this system. We have already had measures enough for increasing the power and patronage of governments, and for promoting the interests of parties; let us now have one great and enlightened and honest measure for the benefit of the youth of Scotland.

Dr Paterson's efforts were not confined to oratory. When his elders were charged to 'see that the children's education be not neglected', it was their ordinary education that was meant. Much work was put towards improving the general educational standards in Kirkwall. He held that only those should be employed who had 'studied teaching as a science and acquired it as an art' – rather than aspirant or failed ministers of the Established Church. During 1847 he wrote that he had been 'prosecuting the educational improvements of the town' via meetings with the Town Council towards the building of an Academy. The creation in 1830 of an Infant School in Kirkwall had also been the fruit of his labours.[9]

In 1896, David Webster wrote that his congregation, 'by its agencies' had 'instructed and trained a vast number of young people in the Christian faith'. In the first edition of the *Record* in January 1880, there were Sabbath Schools (meeting on Sunday evenings) at the Church under his direct Superintendence; a Mission School in Main Street and a further school in Shore Street. Three Sabbath schools controlled by the UP Church met in Tankerness, with others at Scapa and Caldale. In all some 484 children were enrolled in 1880. By January 1886, 583 pupils were on the roll, being taught by 69 teachers. A printed syllabus of topics from the Shorter Catechism and the Bible was provided every quarter in the *Record*, which all schools followed; and from which Mr Webster preached every Sunday morning. Children were set written exercises on the syllabus, and the names of those supplying correct answers were published in the *Record*. In addition, there were annual written examinations on the work of the Schools during the year.

> The infant classes of the Sabbath School met for examination on Wednesday, 29th December, at 12 noon. There were present 45 young people from 5 to 9 years of age. The result of the examination was altogether satisfactory. It was a pleasure to hear the little ones answering so well the questions prescribed, and repeating with accuracy the hymns and passages of scripture. It was gratifying to see so large a number present themselves. The other divisions will observe that their examination has been fixed for the 4th February. Senior Division – First Class – the Shorter Catechism from question 1 to 48; and the quarterly exercises for 1886 on the life of David.

It is obvious from the editions of the *Record* that the Sabbath Schools were close to Mr Webster's heart. 'The importance of this department of Christian work cannot be overestimated,' he wrote in April 1880. He remained convinced of the usefulness of the Shorter Catechism in this work, describing it as 'the cream of Christian doctrine'.

> We have heard objections taken to teaching young people the Shorter Catechism on the ground that it contains so much that is beyond the compass of their understanding. But on the same ground objections might be taken to teaching them the Bible. The Shorter Catechism is but a compendium of what is most essential in Bible truth, and the most admirable of all the compendiums that have ever been written.

On a lighter note, the *Record* notes the annual Sabbath School picnics and soirées, and the innovation of an annual Sabbath Schools' Flower Show by the Kirkwall Sabbath School Union.

> Under the auspices of the Kirkwall Sabbath-schools of all denominations it has been resolved to have a Flower Show on the 27th and 28th of August next. The object is to cultivate a taste among the young for flower growing, which is not only an innocent but an interesting and refining recreation. We hope that the young people connected with our Sabbath Schools will set themselves earnestly to the competition. Though only Sabbath scholars are allowed to compete for prizes, all parties are respectfully invited to send in flowers and plants for exhibition and adjudication.

If the *Record* testified to the UP Congregation's concern for children's work, it also reflects the emphasis put by the entire denomination on Foreign Missions – for the evangelisation of the world. Both a Congregational and a Junior Missionary Society existed, each with its own team of Collectors, in addition to those of the Managers. In 1885, the Accounts show a total of £587 raised for local ministry and a further £219 raised for foreign missionary work. Regular meetings with missionaries on furlough were held. In 1883, Mrs Webster led the movement to create a Ladies' Committee to support the work of Zenana Missions – travelling medical missions to the women of India. 'Women seldom fail in anything they take in hand,' wrote her husband. The Zenana Committee, too, appointed Collectors to visit the congregation's homes twice a year. Further collections were held to build a church for the UP missionary in San Remo, Italy; and to support eight Indian orphans from childhood into adult employment.

For the UP Church, the progress of Christian Mission was part of the spirit of the age, the spiritual side of the era of Empire. In January 1880, Mr Webster made the prediction that 'the whole of our Indian Empire will have been Christianised in little under two centuries'. Mission was considered as an essential part of their individual and collective Christian obedience to the Gospel.

> The maintenance of gospel ordinances among ourselves, as a Christian congregation, is but one-half of our duty: – the extension of it beyond ourselves is the remaining half. And in proportion as we realise this two-fold duty, and carry it into practice do we answer the end of the Church's existence. It follows, then, that in so far as we are a missionary church we are a true church, and no farther . . . the missionary spirit is not something adventitious to our religion, an article of taste or show wherewith to decorate our attire, a chaplet of beauty, or a wreath of laurel with which to decorate its brow, but religion itself. All sections of the Christian church take part . . . in subjugating the world to Christ, and we rejoice to see them vying with each other in gathering immortal honours on the field of conflict with the powers of darkness . . . It is the spirit of faith and prayer . . . that is to convert the world . . .
>
> Our Church has all along been distinguished for her missionary zeal; she has emblazoned on her banner, as her watchword, 'The World for Christ'. At home we have faithfully held fast and held forth the truth as it is in Jesus Christ. We have maintained our distinctive principles and earnestly contended for the Church's right to spiritual freedom and independence. Abroad we have pushed our conquests for Christ in many lands and thousands of souls have been gathered in to the garner of God. To His name be all the glory.

It is obvious that, as with other Presbyterian Churches of the nineteenth century, the leadership role of the minister was central to the life of the congregation. By the close of the nineteenth century, being almost seventy years old, the Rev. David Webster had been minister at the UP Church, Kirkwall, for thirty six years and thirty as sole pastor. It was time for the congregation to appoint an assistant to support him. His had been the task of consolidation – carrying on the work of the famed Dr Paterson into an age of increasing doubt and slackening church discipline. Reading the *Record*, there is a sense of disappointment about some of his articles as the century closed. His Church might once have been named 'The Paterson Kirk', but the less spectacular ministry of Mr Webster – conscientious, kindly, diligent – should not be overlooked. From the successive editions of the *Record* between 1880 and 1899 it is possible to draw together a picture of the daily work of Dr Paterson's colleague and successor. Each year, he reported to the annual business meeting on the pattern and progress of his pastoral ministry.

The January 1882 edition, therefore, recorded the annual meeting of the previous November, at which Mr Webster reported he had 'presided at 38 week-day prayer meetings and paid 913 pastoral visits'. If we allow the minister a fortnight's holiday in the year, he had made some 18 visits a week for fifty weeks during 1880-81. The following table gathers together the factual information printed between 1880 and 1899 about the minister's visiting programme.

Year	*Elders' districts visited*	*Households visited*
1880-81	–	913
1881-82	–	559
1882-83	14	600 'about'
1883-84	12	630
1884-85	10	586
1885-86	9	540
1886-87	7	485
1887-88	12	500 '& over'
1888-89	8	500 'a little under'
1889-90	8	–
1890-98	not given	not given
1898-99	6	–

Over the nine years 1880/81 to 1888/89, it seems that Mr Webster on average visited some 10-12 households per week, with his rate of visiting tending to decline over the years. As a general principle, he devoted Tuesdays to the task of general visitation of Elders' Districts, announcing in advance via the *Record* and by pulpit intimation which

Districts would be seeing him over the quarter. In January 1885, he intimated, 'We now resume the visitation of the town districts, but instead of giving every Tuesday to this routine work as hitherto, we purpose in future to devote every third Tuesday to the visitation of the sick and infirm.' The same principle was still in operation in 1891, when he reported that eight Districts had been visited during 1889-90, and that 'this, with the visitation of the sick, has occupied the best part of two days weekly.'

It should not be thought that David Webster's visits were simply a matter of tea and a chat. During 1883-84, he visited the country Districts belonging to the Kirkwall Church and reported that he had enjoyed their welcome to their minister and the opportunity to pray with his congregation in their homes. In 1886, after visiting the town Districts, he reported:

> These had not been mere formal calls. The young people in the houses visited had been examined in respect to religious knowledge, and earnest and prayerful counsel given. He could not but hope that these short seasons of pastoral intercourse would be blessed both to pastor and people.

Attention to the young people of his families was very much a priority of Mr Webster's. Again in January 1889, he wrote:

> In the district visitations Mr Webster is always glad to meet with the children and examine them a little both on secular and sacred subjects. He does not ask that they should be kept at home from the day school to meet him, but is gratified when they are. It is but once every two years that in this way he can have an opportunity of meeting them.

We may wonder whether children would be pleased or aggrieved at being kept off school in order to be examined (though in a kindly way) by the minister! From this extract we also gather that the minister's routine took him round all the households in membership within the twenty Elders' Districts every two years. The total number of members thus visited varied between 1,200 and 1,100 during the 1880s, tending to decline towards 950 in the late 1890s.

By 1898, looking back in retrospect, he wrote of the aims and principles of his visits, and of the support that the eldership gave in the work of visiting.

> During the year six of the twenty districts into which the congregation is divided have been visited pastorally. The visits thus made have not been mere perfunctory calls, but occasions of Christian counsel, admonition, and prayer. It is a pleasant duty for a pastor to meet with his people in their own homes for a short season's Christian intercourse and as affording an opportunity of examining the young and conversing with them. Specially gratifying and encouraging is it to find evidence of the observance of family religion in the homes of the people. But it is saddening to think that there are homes among us in which there is no family altar and no stated reading of the word of God. Besides our routine district visitations, the sick and the afflicted have required special attention. We have at present a staff of eighteen elders, who are helpers to us in this department of Christian work, and whose visits to their respective districts especially to the sick and aged, are thankfully spoken of.

Apart from visiting, what else was the minister's task? Much time must have been spent in preparation for Sunday duties. The day began with the *Fellowship Meeting for Prayer and Reading the Scriptures in the Session House every Lord's Day morning at 8 o'clock.* Though an elder presided over this Fellowship, it had an important place in the minister's sympathies. Next came the *Young Men's Christian Fellowship Association at half-past 9 o'clock.* The Forenoon Service took place at 11.15 am; and the Afternoon Service at 2.15 pm. Mr Webster was Superintendent of the main Sabbath School that met in the Church at 5.30 pm; and he personally led the *Young Men's Bible Class at 7 o'clock.* This completed his Sabbath duties: his *Young Women's Bible Class* was held on Wednesday evenings.

In his determination to incorporate children and young people into the life of the Church (and perhaps to rationalise preparation?) he normally lectured in the morning service on the Bible passages set for study that day at Sunday School; parents, teachers and children were therefore all expected at the forenoon service. Both morning and afternoon services included a sermon of almost an hour in length. In one *Record*, while explaining the order normally followed in worship, he wrote:

> We have no desire to see the length of the sermon or exposition abridged, and hope the day will never come when this important part of our church service will be relegated to a subordinate place. We have no sympathy with the outcry heard in some quarters (happily not here) for a twenty minutes' discourse. With due preparation and with the earnestness which the nature of his subject demands, the minister of the word will have no difficulty in securing the attention of an audience of average intelligence for forty or fifty minutes, and he can scarcely do justice to his theme in less time than that.

He did acknowledge, however, that length was a matter of what was customary:

> Nor have we any authority save that of experience to guide us in respect of the length of the service. Judging from prevailing practice, it would appear that an hour and half to two hours at most is as long as the attention of the worshipper is likely to be sustained. The spirit may be willing but the flesh is weak.

Preparation of two full services of such length, including that needed for two such sermons each week, must have required a good deal of time in the study. Further time was needed for the other meetings that were part of the congregational routine. During 1881-82, Mr Webster presided at some 118 meetings 'connected with the congregation for prayer, religious instruction and congregational work'. These would include meetings of the Missionary and Temperance Associations – adult and juvenile – that were important elements of congregational life. In 1885-86, the tally rose to 153 'meetings more or less intimately connected with the work of the congregation'; and the next year he reported a total of 156 – three a week, besides Sunday worship, funerals and weddings. In addition to this congregational work, David Webster also found time for his duties to the UP Presbytery of Orkney and to serve on the Kirkwall School Board from 1873 to 1894, and on the St Ola School Board from 1894 to 1897, being Chairman for twelve years.

> At home we have faithfully held fast and held forth the truth as it is in

Jesus Christ. We have maintained our distinctive principles and earnestly contended for the Church's right to spiritual freedom and independence.

To conclude this look at the life and legacy of the Kirkwall Seceder congregation, we concentrate on this phrase: 'distinctive principles'. Several of these we have already covered. This was a congregation that emphasised the importance of personal religion – personal conviction – a personal walk with Christ. The lead article in the January *Record* for 1885 began with these words: *'Am I a Christian or not? There is no question a man can propose to himself of more importance than this – it has bound up in it the interests of eternity. What is it to be a Christian? It is to be a believer in Christ – a follower of Christ; it is to have obtained some measure of likeness to Christ, and to be aiming at complete conformity to His image.'* It is very clear that the Seceders were first and foremost Evangelicals.

They were also Voluntaries: believing that their faith called upon them by their own generosity to sustain the work of their church – to look to no-one else, and certainly not to accept payment or control from the state.

They were a Missionary congregation with a track record of success, within Kirkwall, within Orkney, and in the field of Foreign Missions. Outward-looking and forward-looking: these are also distinctive marks of the UP congregation.

Finally, they had two further characteristics. After the struggles of their very earliest days were over, the UPs were a denomination that looked for Christian unity. Nationally, the United Secession of 1820 was a union of the progressive forces within the Burgher and AntiBurgher Synods.[10] In 1847, the name changed to United Presbyterian when the Relief Church came into the fold. During the 1860s, negotiations took place for union with the Free Church. In Kirkwall, Dr Paterson took a firm line:

> I cannot speak on the side of separation; I cannot speak on the side of sectionalism; I cannot speak on the side of denominationalism: I can only speak on the side of union. No doubt the meaning of this language waits interpretation; but I have thought it carries meaning enough with it to warrant its utterance, and that meaning is, that the Churches of Christ

in our land are in an abnormal and unnatural state, and ought to be brought into a state of union.

Looking through the *Record*, we therefore find that the UP ministers enjoyed good relations with the ministers of other churches working in Kirkwall. When the UP Victoria Street Hall (now the Kirkwall Baptist Church) was opened, both the Cathedral and the Free Church ministers were asked to visit and speak. The King Street Free Church minister, the Rev. Alexander Isdale, was a guest speaker at the Centenary Celebrations: his topic, 'How Christians can best exhibit the Unity of the Spirit.' *'Let Christian people show that they have Christ's cause more at heart than the upkeep of the denomination: that the Gospel comes first and the congregation second,'* he argued.[11]

By 1896, union between the Free and UP Churches was again on the national agenda. The Kirkwall UP congregation, well used to working with their sister church at King Street, were enthusiastically in favour. The youth organisation, the Young People's Guild, had debated the question in 1892.

> The November meeting was occupied by a debate on 'Is the Union of the Scottish Presbyterian Churches practicable?' The discussion was freely entered into by the members, whom this interesting item had drawn out in great numbers, so that the discussion became so spirited that it monopolised the whole time of the meeting to the exclusion of the usual programme of music, readings etc. Needless to say, the almost unanimous voice of the Guild was for union, it being generally understood that union, so far as the Established Church is concerned, must mean its disestablishment and disendowment.[12]

In September 1898 the Session voted in favour of the Union proposals; and finally on February 1899, the congregation at a formal meeting unanimously voted in favour of Union. The national union of the Free and UP Churches took place in 1900, and Kirkwall found itself with two United Free Presbyterian congregations – the Paterson Kirk, and the King Street Kirk.

There is one final note to add: one final 'distinctive characteristic' of the church in the line of the Seceders. These were congregations that believed in the freedom of the church as well as in its unity. They had paid and continued to pay a heavy price to secure that freedom. The 1900 Union was immediately soured when a tiny minority of the Free Church sued to retain the entire property, name and possessions of the denomination. The House of Lords supported them and held that, indeed, the Union violated the Free Church's original constitution, which the Lords believed bound that Church to the Westminster Confession. By allowing ministers and elders freedom of opinion on the non-essential matters of the faith, the Court held that the UF Church had broken away from the Westminster Confession and that it had no power to do so. But the leaders of the UF Church demanded that they be free – free from the control of the State, and free, too, from the claims of history. They served a Living Christ, and claimed the freedom to walk with Him as His Spirit led them.

The acknowledged national leader of the Free side of the Uniting Church was Dr Rainy; he was an eloquent spokesman for this principle of freedom under God.

> We have to maintain as of old the spiritual views of the Church of Christ, the liberty and independence which belong to the Church of Christ, the liberty and independence which are valued because they are necessary to obedience. We cannot obey our Master unless we keep ourselves free to obey Him. If there is anything to which this principle applies, surely it applies to the Confession of Faith. The idea of a Church consenting to be held absolutely and for ever by the faith of men who died two hundred or two hundred and fifty years ago – good men, no doubt – that idea is simply to be denounced as thoroughly ungodly. It is an ungodly idea, and the Church or the tribunal that cherishes it is unawares proceeding on fatally wrong principles. The Christian faith is to believe in a living and present God, a living and present Saviour, a living and a present Holy Spirit, to whom we hold relations while we live and till we die.

The UF Union went ahead, and an Act of Parliament partially reversed the decision of the House of Lords in the Free Church Case. Congregations were given the choice to join the UF, or to remain with the Free Church. In 1900, the Free Church united with the United Presbyterian Church to form the United Free Church. In 1929, the United Free Church joined with the Church of Scotland to create a reunited national church, free from control by the state authorities, funded by the generosity of its members and not by the tithe, in which its congregations call their own ministers. The key organising principles of the Secession had won the day: patronage and state funding and control had been abolished. The Church of Scotland in Orkney inherited most of the buildings and congregations of all three nineteenth century denominations: in some cases that meant three kirks in a single parish. In Kirkwall both the King Street Free Kirk Congregation and the UP Paterson Kirk proceeded into the United Free Church, and thence together into the Church of Scotland after 1929. They united as a single congregation named Kirkwall East Church, in 1968.

The current Church of Scotland in Orkney still uses a good number of buildings erected by congregations not part of the Established Church of the nineteenth century. All over the county can be seen the ruins of 'Auld Kirk' Churches. Indeed, apart from the Cathedral, of the ancient parish church sites only St Ninian's Deerness, St Michael's Harray and Stenness Kirk remain in the possession of the Kirk and in use for weekly Sunday worship. One of the legacies of both the Secession and the Disruption was the multiplication of churches and manses across the landscape. As uniting congregations made their choice of buildings, keeping some and abandoning others, more and more 'peedie kirks' either fell in ruin with their Established predecessors or were put to new uses. Nevertheless, the legacy of the Secession in Orkney is not confined to buildings. It includes the *distinctive principles* of the Secession: a church that held to the gospel of Christ, that supported its work by voluntary giving, an outward-looking and forward-looking church, looking towards greater Christian unity; a church that sought to be free to obey its Lord – free from the state and free from the past. These were its principles – and surely they are or should be our principles as well.

The Rev. Dr William Logie – a minister of the Established Church of Scotland of the first half of the 19th century.[13]

By way of comparison and contrast to the ministers of Kirkwall's UP Church, it is well worth looking at Rev. Dr William Logie, minister first at Lady, Sanday (1811-24), and then of the first charge of St Magnus Cathedral (1824-56). Son of a Kirkwall merchant, 'the best commercial business at that time in Orkney' and heir to the estate of Isbister in Rendall, William Logie followed instead a vocation in the ministry of the Established Church, a ministry after his University and Divinity Hall education in Edinburgh that was exercised entirely within Orkney. His sons followed both his vocation and his interest in medicine, William becoming minister at Firth Parish Church, and James entering a Kirkwall partnership of GPs. This, then, is a minister of a leading Orcadian family – unlike those of the UP Church, who came from outside the county.

Dr Logie's memorial volume was published by Rev. William Logie for the family – much as Dr Paterson's brother produced *his* memorial book. Though an Establishment minister like his father, Rev. William accepts the somewhat negative view held by the UP histories of the Kirk's ministry in Orkney in the early 1800s.[14]

> But previous to the time of which I write, apostolic purity, earnestness, and fidelity had sadly languished and decayed, not only in many of the pulpits of Scotland, but to a great extent throughout all Christendom.

Rev. Dr William Logie, minister, first charge, St Magnus Cathedral, Kirkwall

There were, indeed, in Orkney at that time and previously, some able and exemplary ministers of the Church, who would have done honour to any Church in any age,... But... the warmest friend of the Church, who is also a friend of truth, will readily admit that, at the close of the last century and the commencement of the present, such men were not so numerous as to be lost sight of in the crowd. On the contrary,... a cold, formal and lifeless theology to a great extent occupied the pulpits, and... the lives of not a few of the clergy were either careless, or so openly scandalous as to draw upon them the heaviest ecclesiastical censures...

Dr Logie, from his youth and throughout his ministry, sought to be an 'able and exemplary' minister.

In the light of the criticism of the Established Kirk by the Secession, it comes as some surprise to find that he is described both by his son and in his own writings as 'evangelical'. William wrote of his father:

His views of Divine truth were strictly evangelical, in the true meaning of that much-abused word. He preached to men as sinners, and directed them to the Saviour as their only refuge; he pressed the offers of mercy upon them, with all the earnestness of one who had himself embraced them, and felt their value... He was 'mighty in the Scriptures,' and his most powerful arguments were drawn from that sacred Treasury...

Among Dr Logie's published sermons is that preached by him at the beginning of his ministry at the Cathedral, on 28 November 1824. His text was 'For I determined not to know any thing among you, save Jesus Christ, and Him crucified' [1 Cor.2:2]. Having expounded the text, the new minister went on to state clearly that the 'system of instruction' to be followed by him:

... is the system properly called Evangelical, but to which the world has often affixed the nicknames of Methodism, Calvinism and Enthusiasm. I mention Calvinism, as one of the false appellations applied to that scheme of doctrine and instruction, which ascribes the salvation of man to God's free and sovereign grace, and gives prominence to those truths which relate to a Saviour, and are peculiar to His Gospel...

No 'Moderate', Dr Logie was a firm supporter of the Reformed Faith, 'the evangelical doctrines or doctrines of grace' which he believed originated not solely with Calvin but rather to have been held in common by all the leading Reformation theologians. He believed that, where such doctrines flourished, there also flourished 'purity of national manners . . . the cause of learning . . . civil liberty . . . the noblest developments of human energy, intelligence and virtue.' He treasured the civil and religious liberties of Scotland, gained for his generation by those who stood by the evangelical cause in 'the days of persecution for conscience' sake'.

If William Logie on entering his charge in the Cathedral proposed to preach evangelically, he also informed his congregation that he intended to be a visiting minister, one who honoured the practice of the Church 'in prescribing to her ministers an annual round through the families under her charge . . .' He wrote that, though the duty had fallen in some places into disuse, he believed it had value.

> The importance of this service does not so much depend on the instructions delivered, which are generally very brief and simple, and chiefly addressed to the younger branches, as on the opportunity it affords of reminding both the minister and his flock that the pastoral relationship subsists between him and them not only as a body but as individuals, and of bringing the truths of religion to the bosom of every family and to the heart of every member of the congregation.

He would not visit officiously, he added, but he knew from his time on Sunday that 'good effect' flowed from visitation. Further, he wished it to be known that he saw importance in the visiting of the 'sick and afflicted'. A heart might be 'softened by affliction' and 'if health and strength are restored, the seed sown in sorrow's dark hour may spring up and bring forth fruit to the glory of God and the sinner's salvation'. As a child, William Logie experienced the deaths of seven brothers and sisters; only one sibling besides himself survived to adulthood. His own personal faith in Christ may well have dated from that childhood experience of 'affliction'. Marrying in 1814, Dr Logie was himself to lose four of his six children, two in infancy and two in childhood, between 1826 and 1831.

Further trials were added from 1831. Rev. David Petrie was appointed as his colleague in the second charge of the Cathedral in that year. Though both evangelicals, the two ministers differed sharply over the issue of the time – the relationship between State and Established Church. Whereas Dr Logie believed in constitutional legality, Mr Petrie followed the national leadership of Dr Chalmers in seeking to gain more freedom for the Kirk, if necessary by unilateral action. It was Mr Petrie's supporters who petitioned Presbytery for a new building for the Kirkwall Church; it was Dr Chalmers' Church Extension Committee that helped provide the funds for the East Church of the 1830s. Dr Logie, who opposed the building of the new kirk, therefore experienced in 1841 a local 'disruption', a 'lime and stone disruption' of his own, when Mr Petrie and a section of the St Magnus congregation abandoned him in the old, damp Cathedral. When the critical General Assembly came in 1843, both Kirkwall ministers were present in Edinburgh. Mr Petrie walked out of the Assembly Hall with Dr Chalmers and helped create the Free Church; Dr Logie remained in the Hall and stayed loyal to the Church of Scotland.

> Actuated by that sense of duty which was his ruling principle, he conquered his natural aversion to scenes of excitement and strife, in order to attend the famous General Assembly of 1843, where he witnessed, with deep regret and disapprobation, the retreat of the seceding party. From that Assembly he returned, animated with the zeal of Nehemiah to rebuild the walls of Jerusalem. . . . The Church in Orkney was in a state of collapse, and that apathetic indifference within, which often succeeds a great struggle, was added to active hostility from without . . . for, though only six ministers in full charges seceded, out of a Synod consisting of twenty-one members, yet it so happened that the great majority of those who remained were either wholly or partially disabled by age or infirmity . . . He stood almost alone in the breach, and contemplated, with deep emotion, the rupture of many solemn ties, the alienation of his seceding brethren with whom he had long lived on terms of Christian fellowship. . . . A large and most respectable portion of his congregation, indeed, stood by him, but the alienation of his colleague, and of many of his esteemed flock, who had imbibed Free Church principles, affected him deeply . . .

Mr Petrie and his supporters, already in possession of the East Kirk, initially remained there as Kirkwall's Free Church. The titles to the building, however, belonged to the Established Church, whose national Committee had assisted with the necessary funds to build it. Legal action in the end succeeded in evicting them, by which time Mr Petrie himself had accepted a call to the Free Church in Govan. His congregation continued, building a Church of their own in King Street. In 1893, this was rebuilt – the current King Street Halls.[15]

If legal controversy raged between the Establishment and the Free Church, it was as nothing to that over who rightfully possessed the building and patronage of St Magnus Cathedral. William Logie had been presented by both rival parties – the Crown, and the Kirkwall Burgh Council. At great expense, the case eventually reached the House of Lords in 1830, who ruled in favour of the Council as regards patronage – the right to appoint the ministers.[16] The Crown, however, still claimed ownership of the structure of St Magnus and in 1847 Dr Logie and his congregation were themselves evicted, so that repairs might begin. The Established Congregation therefore moved into the now vacant East Kirk; Dr Logie was not to return to the Cathedral before he died. Rev. William Logie concludes the story:[17]

> Ultimately, the Crown revoked all claim to the Cathedral, in favour of the Town Council and inhabitants, to whom it had been granted by ancient royal charters; and the Presbytery having at last adopted the usual steps for obtaining a parish church, the matter was carried into the Court of Session, and the result was a compromise, – in terms of which the Cathedral was declared the Parish Church, and the Heritors and Council took upon themselves the burden of upholding that vast fabric in all time coming. It was accordingly fitted up in accordance with plans furnished by the courts' architect, Mr Bryce, who is alone responsible for whatever 'Vandalism' may be supposed to have been committed.[18]

When, finally, St Magnus was reopened for worship, the East Kirk was sold, demolished, and its materials used for house-building.

Much of what William Logie wrote of his father might also have been written about either Dr Paterson or David Webster. All three were dedicated and devoted ministers, whose preaching followed similar doctrinal patterns. For example, this could have been written about any of these three . . .

> Every event that befell him and his, – every difficulty or duty, was made a matter of earnest prayer; and he never took any step without asking counsel, and imploring a blessing from on High. He loved his profession; and all its duties were his great pleasures . . .

. . . but it was in fact written of William Logie. It was politics – both the politics of church government and of the national political parties – that divided them. Dr Paterson was a Liberal – even a radical Gladstonian Liberal. He spoke on Party Platforms, was active in electioneering. Dr Logie also had strong political views:

> His political sentiments were clearly defined and firmly maintained. He was a sound and consistent Conservative, and a warm friend of religious and civil liberty. He was not ashamed of his political creed; nor did he ever shrink from publicly supporting the Conservative cause, when duty required him to do so.

William Logie surely had Dr Paterson in mind by way of comparison when he wrote this of his father:

> While he loved labour, he confined himself strictly to the sphere of his profession. He disliked the platform as much as he loved the pulpit. He steadily refused to 'entangle himself with the affairs of this life' . . . Hence, he did not highly approve of the modern fashion of ministers coming prominently forward as public or itinerant lecturers, on subjects unconnected with their profession; or as platform orators or political agitators. He considered that such work, however useful and praiseworthy in itself, should be undertaken by others . . .

Finally, it is worth recording of Dr Logie that, despite the controversies that threatened to entangle his ministry, like his contemporaries in the other Kirkwall churches, he too understood that what united them was ultimately of more importance. '*To the constitutional principles of the Church of Scotland, in doctrine, discipline and government he was most conscientiously attached,*'[19] but in *Services and Sermons* there is a most interesting address given in the Kirkwall Grammar School, 19 October 1851, to a party of twenty two men and women about to emigrate to Australia. The group was denominationally mixed; the Cathedral minister, having exhorted them to continue with a life of prayer and Bible study, and to think of themselves as Christian missionaries, said:

> Be stated in your attendance on the public ordinances of religion. There are ministers in Australia belonging to both the Established Church of Scotland and to other churches, with which some of you are connected. I trust that many of you will find churches within your reach of the kind you prefer; but should it be otherwise, do not on that account neglect the public worship of God. All the churches here are the same in doctrinal belief – they only differ in church government or other externals – only in points which affect not the vitals of religion and, in fact, are not worth separating for, except for the pleasure which some take in keeping up the spirit of party. I am mistaken, if, when you come to that new country, you will not think much less of the points which divide us than you do here; and perhaps you will wonder how men should allow such points to divide them. If the Gospel is preached in your neighbourhood, though not by a preacher of the communion with which you were connected, by all means repair to the House of God, for His presence and blessing are not confined to those of any one denomination.[20]

By the 1850s and 1860s, it is clear that the heat generated first by the Secession and then the Disruption, the conflicts of the first four decades of the nineteenth century, was cooling. Dr Logie's stance of loyalty to both reformed doctrine and the Established Church was part of a general process whereby the Church of Scotland began to regain lost ground and lost friends. Nationally, its percentage of the Presbyterian fold increased from 48% in 1860 to 53% in 1891; the Free Kirk and UP figures were 32% and 30%, and 20% and 17% respectively.[21] Nevertheless, B.H. Hossack's view in 1900 was that 'Dissent is now dominant in Kirkwall'.[22] Dr Logie's ministry was a matter of conducting a rearguard action on two fronts at once. Perhaps because the popular memory has forgotten him in preference for Dr Paterson, let us give Dr Logie a final word – the ending of his 1851 address to the emigrants:

'Finally, brethren and sisters, dear country-men and women, farewell. Be perfect, be of good comfort, be of one mind, live in peace, and the God of love and peace shall be with you.' Amen and Amen.

It is clear that I find myself much in sympathy both with the UP church and with Dr Logie! The UP concept of Christianity as a 'religion of progress', however, is not one that is in tune with the contemporary mood. Rather, the church seems to represent something from the past, somewhat marginal to the spirit of this age. Perhaps it is significant that the part of my ministry in Orkney most accessible to the general community was historical.

The spirit of the nineteenth century was one that believed that God was leading his people to something new and better – that evangelical truth was reforming society on a world-wide basis. This view was held in common by Drs Paterson, Logie and others. Before 1840, one Orkney minister was able to write:[23]

> If Christianity has improved Man in the ages that are past, can we doubt that it will do so in those that are to come? At some future period, every heart will be united in love to Christ, and in Christian love. A portion of frailty will adhere to human nature; for Man cannot cease to be man: but the grosser vices will be diminished: – Envy, malice and jealousy, may no longer poison the sources of domestic joy, nor mad ambition deluge the world with blood: for our children or our children's children may be reserved a degree of perfection in piety, wisdom, benevolence, and happiness, compared to which our present condition is only a state of childhood and barbarity.

In Europe, the vision was shattered on the battlefields of two World Wars and the cynicism of the Cold War. In the church, the constant loss of membership, increasing financial pressures, theological uncertainty and the secularity of the media drain hope away.[24] But our faith should have hope – together with faith and love – at its centre. Somehow in this new century, we need to recapture this Biblical emphasis.

The nineteenth century saw major debates on church unity: the Presbyterian denominations slowly attempting to find a way to come together again. I find impressive the way they were (after 1850) prepared to recognise each other as Christians with a valid part, under God, to play. Reunion meant much to them. Reunion in the end required the Established Church to surrender much of its former constitutional position, required it to accept that the Free Church had been correct to insist on the abolition of patronage. Reunion also required the UP/UF Church to surrender its independence in a larger union. Working together with other Christians and between denominations in the future will no doubt ask for similar sacrifices.

Public debates on the future of church buildings in Orkney can be so very backward looking. Thinking of the Cathedral as a 'spiritual building' (whatever that is!) the Council's Committee appears to have its mind focused on the historicity of the structure; changes to accommodate a living Christian tradition are not easily accepted. Similarly, a debate raged for several years about the intention of the East Kirk congregational leadership to abandon Dr Paterson's building with its seating for 1400 in favour of a renovated King Street Church. Letters to the *Orcadian* have argued that the heritage of the Paterson Kirk is being betrayed. What, however, appears to be forgotten is that the people of the Paterson Kirk of the nineteenth century believed in a principle of progress – of demolition and building and alteration in order to suit the spiritual needs of the congregation. They gave priority to spiritual priorities – the spirituality of people – well ahead of preserving a heritage in stones and glass.

The principles proclaimed by Dr Rainy also still need attention. The Church in each generation must be free to follow her Lord, because obedience to the Lord is crucial to Christian living. She cannot be trapped in a historical time-warp – whether one constructed of man-made theology or one of man-made buildings. In my last year as Community Minister in Orkney, I found myself preaching on a number of occasions from Isaiah 43:14-21.

> Thus says the LORD, your Redeemer, the Holy One of Israel: . . . Do not remember the former things, or consider the things of old. I am about to do a new thing; now it springs forth, do you not perceive it? I will make a way in the wilderness and rivers in the desert.

Church History has its uses – it helps us see how Christians have sought to follow their Lord in different circumstances so that we can learn from them. It also has its dangers – that, by looking at history, we should allow our predecessors to dictate to us how we should follow Jesus in our generation. The Jews in exile, seemingly far from hope, were told to remember what their God had done in the past – bringing their forefathers out of Egypt. On that basis, they were urged to put their trust in a God who could and would do new things, bringing living water from the dry desert.

One theme of this book has been the newness of God to different generations of Christians in Orkney – the newnesses of the Celtic Church, the Reformation, the Secession churches – each finding a way to express Christian faith in a way appropriate to their own age and comprehensible to their culture. It has happened before – it can happen again; but it will be new. It needs spiritually renewed people – people with the courage of the monk-voyagers, with the Reformation's love of the Bible, with the forward-looking mentality of the Secession and the loyalty and steadfastness displayed by William Logie.

1 During May 1996, the East Church congregation in Kirkwall celebrated its second century with a variety of special activities including a visit from the former Moderator of the General Assembly, the Very Rev. James Simpson, then minister at Dornoch. The Kirk Session asked me to prepare and give a talk on the historical significance of the congregation in Kirkwall. Not that Kirkwall people need the importance of the 'Paterson Kirk' explained. The second minister of this Secession congregation, Rev. Dr Robert Paterson, had an influential role in Orkney life at the beginning of Victoria's reign. 'The Paterson Kirk' is one of the town's main landmarks, an excellent auditorium built to seat 1400 people. As I did the necessary reading in preparation, I was struck how well words and opinions from this kirk had been preserved from last century. From its early days the congregation had published a quarterly *Record* – and bound copies were available. Besides, Dr Paterson's brother had produced a Biography, using the minister's diaries and papers; and the third minister, David Webster, had written a History of his own following the first centenary celebrations. The talk I gave therefore attempted to allow the people to speak for themselves as much as possible, by using extensive quotations. When it came to the night, I was delighted that with the help of three members of the congregation, suitably dressed, we were able to welcome as our guests 'Dr Paterson', 'Mr Webster' and an 'elder of the kirk' to tell their own story. Finally, the current East Kirk minister, Rev. Allan McCafferty, took the part of an influential Moderator of the Free and United Free Kirks, Dr Robert Rainy. The version of the talk given here

preserves the style of frequent quotations, and also incorporates a short article on 'The Minister's Task' that was written for the same celebrations. A final section has been added that, by way of contrast and so that the Established Church is not altogether overlooked, compares Dr Paterson with his contemporary in the first charge at St Magnus, the Rev. Dr William Logie. This chapter is largely based on the following: *Quarterly Record of the United Presbyterian Church, Kirkwall* – bound edition from January 1880 to October 1899; Rev. John Paterson, *Memoir of Robert Paterson, D.D., Kirkwall* (Edinburgh, 1874); Rev David Webster, *The History of the Kirkwall United Presbyterian Congregation* (Kirkwall, 1910); Rev. Robert Small D.D., *History of the Congregations of the United Presbyterian Church 1733-1900* (Edinburgh, 1904).

2 J.H.S. Burleigh, *A Church History of Scotland* (OUP, 1960) has a most useful flow-chart illustrating the divisions and reunions of the Scottish churches.
3 W.M. Gibson, *Auld Peedie Kirks* (Kirkwall, 1991).
4 All information in this paragraph is taken from Rev. Robert Small D.D., op.cit. vol. ii (1904).
5 Callum Brown, *The Social History of Religion in Scotland since 1730* (London, 1987) pp. 60-70, commenting on an 1891 survey.
6 ed. D.W. Bebbington, *The Baptists in Scotland – a History* (The Baptist Union of Scotland, Glasgow, 1988) pp. 317-20.
7 B.H. Hossack, *Kirkwall in the Orkneys* (Kirkwall 1900 and 1986) pp. 364, 459.
8 Dr Paterson did, however, reject the idea of 'progress' in Christian theology. That was given once for all by Revelation. 'The Gospel Ministry – A sermon by the Rev. Robert Paterson, D.D., preached in the United Presbyterian Church, Kirkwall, on the 24th October 1869, being the First Day of the Fiftieth year of his ministry', (Kirkwall n.d.) p.36: *'We readily and gladly admit that this is an age of progress; . . . But what of all this? The Gospel is not a discovery, it is revelation . . . It has been communicated by God to us, and is perfect – admitting neither progress nor change.'*
9 Mrs Elsa Rendall, M.A., *The Kirk on Westray (The story of the Church of Scotland)* (Kirkwall, n.d.): the first Secession minister on Westray, Mr Reid, is also remembered for his emphasis on education.
10 J.H.S.Burleigh, op. cit. explains in detail the Burgher and AntiBurgher divisions in both Secession denominations: pp. 323-4.
11 In the *Biographical Notice and Memorial Addresses on the death of Rev. Dr. Paterson* (Kirkwall, March 1870) is printed the interesting testimony of an earlier Free Church Minister, Rev. James Stuart. It is well worth reprinting in full. The two men had spent the day together discussing the affairs of the Bible Society. In a mood of mutual confidence, Dr Paterson spoke to the young minister.

> He recounted what he had done and what he wished to do for the good of Kirkwall; how he endeavoured to have cottages erected to remedy the overcrowding which is working so much mischief in our town; how he sought to establish schools and classes to elevate the people; at the same time encouraging me to follow his footsteps, and to cooperate in every good work.

On my stating that this had been my determination all along, his eye kindled with a brightness all its own, and, with a tone of pathos that I shall not forget, he said 'The good of Kirkwall is one of the great objects of my life'; and, said he, and his words were weighty words, 'What have we to gain, and how much has the good cause to lose by sectarian strife? The United Presbyterian congregation in Kirkwall has taken its position; it may be naturally expected to retain it. The Free Church has also taken its position; it will also naturally retain it. The Established Church has taken its position; it, too, will probably retain it. Strife of sects cannot alter the relative position of these bodies, but may hinder the influence of all of them for good.' These words are worth writing in letters of gold, or, better still, we should have them deeply engraven on the tables of our hearts.

12 'Disestablishment and Disendowment' was a slogan of the time. The Orkney Room of the Kirkwall Public Library contains a bound volume entitled *Disestablishment and Disendowment of the Church of Scotland*, being a series of articles produced by 'a member of the Orkney Disestablishment Association', from 1875.

13 My source for what follows is ed. William Logie, *Services and Sermons* published with a memorial to Dr Logie by his son Rev. William Logie, c. 1860. He features in H.W.M. Cant, 'Some aspects of the nineteenth century' in ed. Cant/Firth, op.cit (1989).

14 Here Mr Logie mentions Rev. Gavin Hamilton of Hoy and Graemsay, inducted 1796. Rev. and Mrs Hamilton were also commended by Haldane at the time of his mission to Orkney: B.H. Hossack, op.cit. p. 451. By 1891, Hoy was the only parish in Orkney where the Established Church's members were the majority denomination.

15 B.H. Hossack, op.cit. p. 455-7.

16 Ibid, p. 455.

17 *Services and Sermons* pp.xl, xli.

18 Of course the story did not quite end there. The Town Council having had St Magnus confirmed as Kirkwall's parish kirk and with their right to present the ministers of the Cathedral acknowledged, the magistrates also took over responsibility for the fabric. Patronage, however, was legally abolished in Scotland in 1872 leaving the Council with no rights over the congregation, and yet still responsible for the fabric. The position remains anomalous to this day, Orkney Islands Council having taken over the duties of the Burgh Council.

19 *Services and Sermons* pp. l and li.

20 Dr Logie, however, cautioned his hearers against the Roman Catholic Church. He was a very firmly Protestant minister.

21 Callum Brown, op.cit. p. 65.

22 B.H. Hossack, op.cit. p. 250 – § footnote. The situation is different in today's Orkney. The 1994 Church census showed some 75% of the church-going population of Orkney in membership with the Church of Scotland. Next in size was the Roman Catholic Church, and then the Independent Brethren and Christian Fellowship congregations, taken together. (Minutes of the Church of Scotland Presbytery of

Orkney, 4 February 1997).
23 The Rev. Walter Traill of Westove, *Discourses on the Characteristics of Genuine Christianity* (Edinburgh, 1839). Mr Traill was minister of Sanday: Ladykirk.
24 Gordon Donaldson, *Faith of the Scots* (London, 1990) p.146 expresses the view that it is no part of Christianity to offer hope of continuous progress, and argues that the power of evil over humanity continues from age to age.

INDEX OF PEOPLE

This index does not include references contained within the 'Tables of the Reformed Ministry in Orkney, 1560–1590'

Adam, of Bremen 37, 38
Adomnán, Abbot of Iona 12, 13, 15
Aed, King of Picts 17
Anderson, John 64
Anderson, David 65
Annand, Mr James 60, 61, 62, 63, 64, 66, 68

Baikie, family of Tankerness 79
Balfour, Alison 73
Balfour, Gilbert 66, 72
Beanston, Mr Thomas 60
Bede, the Venerable 15
Bellenden, Sir John of Auchnoule, Justice-Clerk 65, 67
Bellenden, Patrick 67, 72
Ben, Jo. 70
Benedict, of Nursia, St. 16
Bothwell, Bishop Adam of Orkney 56, 57, 58, 59, 60, 63, 64, 65, 66, 67, 72, 83
Bothwell, Francis 60, 63, 64
Brand, Rev. John 70, 81, 82, 83
Brendan, the Voyager 12
Bridei, King of Picts 12, 17
Broadfoot, William 105
Brown, George Mackay 10
Brown, William 62, 65
Bruce, Mr Donald 61
Buchanan, David 106

Callender, Alexander 67
Callender, Andrew, 67
Ceolfrid, Abbot of Wearmouth 15
Chalmers, Rev. Dr Thomas 132
Charles II, King 78
Cheyne, Mr Alex 67
Cheyne, Robert 64
Columba, Abbot of Iona, St. 9, 10, 11, 12, 13, 16, 18, 19, 22, 24, 25, 33, 41
Colville, Harry 67, 68, 73
Cook, Mr James 67
Cormac 12, 19, 22
Craigie, Nicol 60, 61, 65
Cromwell, Oliver, Lord Protector 78
Cumming, James 113
Curitán (Bishop Boniface) 15, 22, 35

David I, King of Scots 42
Davidson, John 68, 69, 88
Dick, Mr Alexander 63, 64
Dicuil 13, 33
Douglas, James Earl of Morton 68
Duncanson, Mr John 65

Elizabeth, Queen of England 55
Erlend, Earl of Orkney 38
Erskine, Ebenezer 103

Finney, Charles 108
Fleming, Thomas 62
Foulsie, Mr Gilbert 61, 63, 64, 66

Gladstone, William Ewart 114
Graham, Bishop George 75

Hakon, King of Norway 19
Hakon Paulsson, Earl of Orkney 39, 40
Halcro, Mr Magnus 63, 64, 72
Halcro, Mr Ninian 63, 67
Halcro, Hugh younger of that ilk 71
Haldane, James 110
Henderson, Cuthbert 67
Henderson, William 67
Henry, Bishop of Orkney 38
Houston, Mr John 64, 65, 71
Houston, Mr Peter 63, 64

Ingster, Edward 62, 65
Isdale, Rev. Alexander 126

James VI, King 74
James VII, King 78, 79

Kaa, James 55
Kerr, Andrew 80
Knox, John 77

Laughton, William 112
Law, Bishop James 74, 75, 77, 83
Logie, James 129
Logie, Rev. Dr William 129, 130, 131, 132, 133, 134, 135, 136, 138
Logie, Rev. William junior 12
Lyon, Rev. James 79, 80

Magnus Paulsson, Earl of Orkney, St. 19, 39, 40, 41, 42, 43
Malison, John 65
Mary, of Guise, Regent of Scotland 55, 72
Mary, Queen of Scots 55, 56, 66
Maxwell, Mr James 62, 63, 64, 65, 66
Melville, Andrew 69
Molyson, John 62

Moodie, Adam 72
Moodie, Mr William 62, 71, 72

Nechtan, King of Picts 15
Ninian, St. 9, 10, 11, 19, 20, 21, 22

Olaf Tryggvasson, King of Norway 35, 36

Papley, Thomas 73
Paterson, Dr Robert 102, 105, 107, 108, 109, 110, 115, 116, 117, 120, 125, 129, 133, 134, 135, 136, 137
Paul, Earl of Orkney 38
Pierson, Mr William 63, 64, 65
Petrie, Rev. David 132, 133
Pettigrew, John 106

Rainy, Dr Robert 127, 137
Ramsay, Duncan 62, 65
Rattray, Thomas 61, 62, 65
Reid, Archibald 61, 62
Reid, Bishop Robert 50, 52, 54, 55, 58, 83
Robertson, James 112, 113
Rognvald, Earl of Orkney 39, 43

Sadler, John 61
Sigurd the Mighty, Earl of Orkney 33, 35, 36
Sigurd, King of Norway 42
Sinclair, David of Hunto 64
Sinclair, Edward of Strome 58, 59, 72
Sinclair, Henry 58
Sinclair, Oliver of Pitcairns 58, 59, 65
Sinclair, Robert 58, 59
Smith, William 62
Stevenson, Thomas 61
Stewart, James Earl of Moray Regent of Scotland 66
Stewart, James 67
Stewart, John 62, 66
Stewart, Patrick Earl of Orkney 70, 73, 74, 75

Stewart, Robert Earl of Orkney
   66, 67, 72
Stewart, Robert   62, 65, 67
Strang, Andrew   71
Strang, Magnus   63, 64
Swinton, Thomas   73

Tailor, Thomas   62
Taylor, William   106
Thorfinn II the Mighty, Earl of Orkney
   37, 38
Thorolf, Bishop of Orkney   37
Thorstein the Red   33
Traill, Mr of Hobbister   115
Triduana, St.   35, 41
Tulloch, James   65
Tulloch, Mr Jerome   61, 62, 65, 68
Tulloch, William   110

Wallace, Adam   54, 55
Walker, Mr Donald   62
Watt, Gavin   61, 65
Webster, Rev. David   101, 106, 107, 108,
   109, 112, 113, 114, 116, 118, 119, 120,
   121, 122, 123, 124, 133
Webster, Mrs David   119
White, John   112
William the Lion, King of Scots   49
William the Old, Bishop of Orkney   39, 40
Willison, Rev. Archibald   106
Wilson, Rev. John   79

Young, Laurence   62, 65

INDEX OF PLACES

This index does not include references to parishes contained within the 'Tables of the Reformed Ministry in Orkney, 1560–1590'

Birsay   18, 19, 25, 34, 37, 38, 39, 40, 50, 51, 52, 58, 62, 64, 65, 66, 67, 69, 81, 87, 105, 106
Burray   52, 53, 60, 62, 63, 67, 81, 105, 110
Copinsay   81
Damsay   81
Deerness   17, 19, 21, 22, 23, 25, 36, 38, 40, 50, 52, 53, 61, 62, 63, 65, 67, 79, 81, 128
Eday   50, 51, 52, 59, 60, 62, 67, 82, 105, 110
Egilsay   39, 50, 51, 54, 60, 62, 63, 68, 82, 106
Evie   50, 51, 52, 54, 60, 62, 65, 66, 68, 81
Eynhallow   17, 35, 38, 54, 62, 68, 82
Faray   62, 82
Firth   50, 51, 52, 61, 68, 73, 81, 105, 129
Flotta   23, 50, 52, 53, 60, 62, 65, 72, 81, 110
Gairsay   62, 81
Graemsay   62, 72, 76, 81
Harray   51, 52, 62, 63, 64, 65, 67, 69, 81, 128
Holm   50, 52, 53, 60, 61, 62, 63, 67, 81, 105, 106
Hoy   12, 52, 53, 54, 60, 62, 72, 76, 81, 87
Kirkwall   6, 13, 19, 40, 43, 52, 54, 57, 61, 63, 64, 67, 71, 73, 75, 79, 80, 81, 83, 84, 85, 86, 87, 101, 103, 104, 105, 106, 107, 108, 110, 113, 114, 117, 118, 119, 120, 122, 124, 125, 126, 128, 129, 132, 133, 134, 135
Lambholm   81
North Ronaldsay   21, 51, 52, 60, 62, 63, 67, 68, 70, 78, 82, 86, 110
Orphir   36, 40, 51, 52, 54, 61, 68, 73, 81
Papa Stronsay   62
Papa Westray (Papay)   1, 16, 17, 18, 22, 33, 35, 38, 40, 41, 50, 51, 52, 60, 62, 63, 68, 82
Rendall   50, 51, 52, 54, 60, 62, 65, 66, 68, 81, 106, 129
Rousay   19, 35, 50, 51, 52, 54, 58, 60, 62, 63, 65, 67, 68, 82, 87, 105
St. Andrews (parish in Orkney)   50, 52, 53, 61, 63, 65, 67, 71, 81
St Magnus Cathedral   4, 40, 41, 43, 50, 53, 54, 57, 59, 63, 64, 65, 68, 71, 72, 73, 79, 80, 82, 83, 85, 101, 103, 129, 130, 131, 132, 133, 135, 137

St Ola (parish in Orkney) 50, 52, 61, 81, 124
Sanday 18, 19, 34, 51, 52, 54, 60, 62, 63, 67, 68, 82, 86, 105, 107, 110, 129
Sandwick 50, 51, 52, 62, 68, 69, 76, 81, 87, 105
Shapinsay 50, 51, 52, 60, 61, 62, 70, 76, 81, 105
South Ronaldsay 19, 21, 52, 53, 60, 61, 62, 63, 65, 67, 70, 71, 81, 105, 110
Stenness 18, 51, 52, 61, 68, 73, 81, 128
Stromness 51, 52, 62, 65, 68, 69, 76, 81, 85, 105
Stronsay 12, 50, 51, 52, 54, 60, 62, 63, 64, 65, 66, 67, 70, 82, 105, 106
Walls (Waas) 19, 52, 53, 60, 62, 72, 76, 81
Westray 12, 36, 40, 50, 51, 52, 60, 62, 63, 65, 66, 68, 70, 82, 105, 110
Wyre 36, 40, 54, 62, 63, 68, 82